C.M.Leve
2727411

STUDIES IN ROMANCE LANGUAGES: 41
John E. Keller, Editor

Gonzalo de Berceo

❖ *Miracles of Our Lady*

Translated by
Richard Terry Mount
and
Annette Grant Cash

THE UNIVERSITY PRESS OF KENTUCKY

Publication of this volume was made possible in part by grants
from The Program for Cultural Cooperation between Spain's
Ministry of Culture and United States Universities, the
University of North Carolina at Wilmington, and the National
Endowment for the Humanities.

Scholarly publisher for the Commonwealth,
serving Bellarmine College, Berea College, Centre
College of Kentucky, Eastern Kentucky University,
The Filson Club Historical Society, Georgetown College,
Kentucky Historical Society, Kentucky State University,
Morehead State University, Murray State University,
Northern Kentucky University, Transylvania University,
University of Kentucky, University of Louisville,
and Western Kentucky University.

Editorial and Sales Offices: The University Press of Kentucky
663 South Limestone Street, Lexington, Kentucky 40508-4008

01 00 99 98 97   5 4 3 2 1

Library of Congress Cataloging-in-Publication Data

Berceo, Gonzalo de, 13th cent.
    [Milagros de Nuestra Señora. English]
    Miracles of Our Lady / Gonzalo de Berceo ; translated from the
Spanish with an introduction by Richard Terry Mount and
Annette Grant Cash.
        p. cm. — (Studies in Romance languages ; 41)
    Includes bibliographical references (p.   ).
    ISBN 0-8131-2019-5 (alk. paper)
    1. Mary, Blessed Virgin, Saint—Poetry. 2. Religious poetry,
Spanish—Translations into English. I. Mount, Richard Terry,
1944– . II. Cash, Annette Grant, 1943– . III. Title. IV. Series:
Studies in Romance languages (Lexington, Ky.) ; 41.
PQ6397.M513 1997
861'.1—dc21   97–2119

This book is printed on acid-free recycled paper meeting
the requirements of the American National Standard
for Permanence of Paper for Printed Library Materials.

Manufactured in the United States of America

◆ To John E. Keller, our mentor and friend

Contents

Foreword

WE ARE FORTUNATE to have at last a translation into English of Gonzalo de Berceo's *Milagros de Nuestra Señora*, and in passing, we have a right to wonder why though the two other most studied works of the Spanish Middle Ages have been in translated form for decades the *Milagros* have not been. There are at least four translations of the *Libro de buen amor* of the fourteenth-century Juan Ruiz, Archpriest of Hita; and at least three of Don Juan Manuel's *El Conde Lucanor*, also of the fourteenth century, are available. Both have been edited several times by scholars of note.

Berceo wrote exclusively, save for one very short poem, in the poetic form we know variously as *cuaderna vía*, the fourfold way, and as *mester de clerecía*. The first reference to this form in Spanish, a brief description actually, appears in the *Libro de Alexandre*, the epiclike life of Alexander the Great. And since Berceo may be the author of the *Alexandre*, as Dana Nelson seems to be proving, then Berceo may have written this passage, which I offer here in translation:

> I use a handsome meter, it is not the minstrel's,
> It is a *mester* without fault, for it is of the clergy;
> It tells a rhymed tale through the fourfold way,
> In counted syllables which is a great skill.

Berceo is the first writer whose name we know to write the Blessed Virgin's miracles in Castilian; the first to claim that he used the language of the people rather than the language of the learned, and the first to include a living miracle, since Miracle 25 deals with one which took place in his own time and place and is found in no other collection of miracles. He wrote in his *Life of St. Dominic of Silos* the following quatrain to drive this point home:

I want to write a piece in polished Romance,
In which the people are accustomed to speak to their
    neighbors,
For I am not learned enough to write one in Latin.
It would indeed be worth, as I believe, a glass of good wine.

Surely these lines prove that he regarded the Spanish vernacular, since *roman paladino* (polished romance) meant to him good Spanish as opposed to Latin, as best suited to the establishment of rapport with his public. This poetic medium, in a way, bridged the void between folk poetry, as represented by the epiclike *mester de juglaría* of the bards, and the poetry of the literate and the erudite. It could be read, of course by the learned reader, but since its poetic form was written in language understandable among the illiterate, it could be enjoyed, when read or recited, by such people.

None of this implies that *cuaderna vía* was a perfect poetic medium or that Berceo's verses were as literary and sprightly as those of Juan Ruiz, who improved upon thirteenth-century forms and made his work a book of recreational reading rather than one as pietistic in intent as Berceo's. Readers will recall that *cuaderna vía* consists of fully rhymed quatrains, whose lines are fourteen syllables divided into two laisses or hemistichs of seven syllables separated by a caesura. Critics, ever since Spanish literature has been studied, have considered it monotonous and therefore dull. In an earlier publication I treated Berceo's medium as follows, and I believe that his original readers would have agreed with me that it was the best of all possible meters: "The full rhyme of *cuaderna vía*'s quatrains has power. It catches the reader in its net and carries him along with force and sometimes with violence. Once entrapped, once caught up in the metrics and trained to march to the regular and unchanging cadence, once taught to expect each line in each quatrain to rhyme completely with each of the other lines, the reader surrenders to *cuaderna vía*'s spell and reads on tirelessly."*

The present translation succeeds in the difficult task of avoiding the literal while maintaining the meaning of it, so as to make Berceo read for a modern audience. The translators quite cor-

---

*Gonzalo de Berceo 38, reprinted as "Cuaderna Vía and Its Appeal," Collectanea Hispanica: Folklore and Brief Narrative Studies by John Esten Keller, ed. Dennis P. Seniff with the assistance of María Isabel Montoya Ramírez (Newark, Delaware: Juan de la Cuesta, 1987), 79.

rectly assume that their readers will agree with them that the lack of literalness will in no way lessen the translation's acceptance. The translators believe, as do I, that a translation should render the ideas and imageries of the original language in the second language with as few changes in meaning, thought, and concept as possible. They have taken little liberty with the Spanish, but have chosen to follow the most modern parlance in order to enhance readability; their intent and their hope has been to make an important work of the past live in the present, maintaining historical perspective, but presenting the original in a style pleasing to their readers throughout the English world, a style, of course, which manages to preserve an attractive "antique" flavor. I believe that they have succeeded in making Berceo speak as clearly and naturally to our century as he spoke to people in his. This translation, then, should appeal not only to specialists, comparatists, folklorists, and scholars in other areas, but also to those in the general public who like to read great works.

The genre of the miracle in literature and folklore, so assiduously studied today, has become a respected area of research. Berceo's miracle stories most definitely belong to this genre and represent along with King Alfonso's *Cantigas de Santa Maria* (best termed in English *The Canticles of Holy Mary*), an apogee of miracle literature written in Spanish.

It is well known that collaboration in translating can greatly enhance such work: collaboration provides for mutual corrections and skills; it stimulates interest and industry and perseverance; and it permits and encourages different approaches and thinking. The translation by Annette Grant Cash and Richard Terry Mount exemplifies the ideals and advantages of complete cooperation and equal responsibility.

This first complete translation of the *Milagros de Nuestra Señora* makes a timely and needed contribution to scholars and the educated general public.

—JOHN E. KELLER

Acknowledgments

WE GRATEFULLY EXPRESS our appreciation to people and institutions without whose help we could not have completed our translation of Berceo's *Milagros*. In 1990, we were participants in a National Endowment for the Humanities summer institute, "Alfonsine Contributions to Medieval Spanish Literature and Culture," directed by John E. Keller and Aníbal Biglieri at the University of Kentucky. There we agreed to begin work on this translation. In the summer of 1993, in another NEH institute, "Translation Theory from the Bible to Benjamin and Beyond," directed by Marilyn Gaddis Rose and Joanna Bankier at SUNY Binghamton, we finished and polished our work. We are very appreciative of the help we received in Binghamton from other translators in our afternoon work sessions and from Beverly Mitchell, another participant, who spent several hours reading and listening to our translations and offered many insightful suggestions. The enthusiastic reaction to our presentation of two of the miracles at the final recital of this institute gave us much encouragement and to members of that audience we are grateful.

Our special thanks to John Keller for his counsel and inspirational example over these many years, to Mary Gillis who served as our copy editor, and to Joann McFerran Mount who proofread the final drafts. We thank them all for their advice and many useful suggestions.

While we were away at the institutes, our families took over our responsibilities and have offered constant encouragement and support throughout this project. We are very much in their debt.

In addition, the College of Arts and Sciences of the University of North Carolina at Wilmington generously gave a research grant, course release time, and special support for the publication of this volume. The translators and the University Press of Kentucky are also grateful to the Program for Cultural Cooperation between Spain's Ministry of Culture and United States' Universities for its support of this project.

Translators' Introduction

Berceo and the Scholar's Art

GONZALO DE BERCEO, the first important Spanish poet known to us by name, was born in the La Rioja region of northeastern Castile in the last years of the twelfth century. He was an elder contemporary of the great learned king Alfonso X the Wise of Castile and, like Alfonso—who produced the multifaceted Galician-Portuguese collection of Marian miracles, *Canticles of Holy Mary (Cantigas de Santa Maria)*—he wrote a collection of miracles of the Virgin Mary (*Miracles of Our Lady*), the first such collection written in Castilian.

Berceo wrote in the erudite poetic form of *cuaderna vía* (fourfold way), a form derived from a similar medieval Latin verse and utilized by the writers of the *mester de clerecía* (scholars' art). This poetry was didactic and developed through French cultural influence in monasteries and emerging universities such as the Estudio General de Palencia, which was established in the year 1212 by Bishop Tello Téllez de Meneses and King Alfonso VIII of Castile. The poetry of the *mester de clerecía* is characterized by monorhymed quatrains with a caesura in the middle of each fourteen-syllable line. The rhyme is consonantal.

In general, the subject matter of the *mester de clerecía* is learned and/or religious. It has traditionally been viewed as entirely distinct from the *mester de juglaría* (minstrels' art),[1] which consists predominantly of sixteen-syllable lines with assonant rhyme, treats nonlearned or popular themes (such as those found in the national epics), and is closely related to the Spanish ballad tradition. However, in recent years, as the question of *clerecía* versus *juglaría* has been reevaluated, the division is no longer so strictly maintained. Uria Maqua says that the border between the two *mesteres* is becoming less and less distinct and the inclusion of certain poems in one *mester* or the other has become more and more debatable (180). Colin Smith, for example, has argued that the author of the *Poem of the Cid* could not have been an itinerant, illiterate minstrel, but—judging by the artistic nature of the poem, its erudite details, and written form—had to have been a man of learning (41). By the same token, there are many *juglaría* elements in the works of *clerecía* and especially in those of Berceo. Germán Orduña long ago suggested that the *mester de clerecía* is a continuation or offshoot of the *mester de juglaría*, which employs the well-proven techniques of the latter: oral presentation, direct address, picturesque details and digressions, use of popular speech and proverbs, and so forth (24-25).

Thus, that his poetry is learned does not at all preclude the fact that Berceo attempted to address a broad spectrum of society. Indeed, his purpose was to offer a learned, and therefore authoritative, form of poetry in the vernacular rather than in Latin and to reach his audience in a style attractive for its themes, images, popular speech, and familiar proverbs. Upon stating his purpose in the fourth strophe of the *Vida de Santo Domingo de Silos* (*Life of St. Dominic of Silos*), Berceo identifies himself and his work, though erudite, with the popular:

I wish to write in plain romance[2]
in which the people are accustomed to talking to their neighbors,
for I am not lettered enough to do another in Latin.
I believe it will be well worth a glass of good wine.

In the last line of this often-quoted quatrain, Berceo places himself within the minstrel tradition, since it was customary for the performer to ask for a drink after a long recitation (Keller *Gonzalo de Berceo* 28). He felt certain that his effort would be worth that traditional glass of wine.

Francisco Rico suggests that Berceo is both simple and sagacious, the embodiment of the duality of the model scholar-cleric described by Diego García de Campos, chancellor to Alfonso VIII, who exhorts clerics to be as harmless as doves and as wise as serpents (6-8; 146-47). Viewing him in this light, the modern reader sees a modesty in Berceo which, whether sincere or contrived, places him through his work—and in spite of his great learning and skill—on the level of his audience, enabling him to establish rapport in the tradition of the *juglares* and more effectively to persuade the audience of his message.

Although Berceo was concerned primarily with religious subjects in his writing, the *cuaderna vía* was in other writers the vehicle for learned narratives on both national and classical themes. Of the more significant poems in *cuaderna vía* (in addition to the works of Berceo) are *Libro de Apolonio* (*Book of Apolonius*, thirteenth century), *Poema de Fernán González* (*Poem of Fernán González*, thirteenth century), *Libro de Alexandre* (*Book of Alexander*, thirteenth century, thought by some to have been written by Berceo),[3] Juan Ruiz's *Libro de buen amor* (*Book of Good Love*, fourteenth century), and Pero López de Ayala's *Rimado de Palacio* (*Palace Poem*, ca. 1400).

Berceo and His Works

What we know about Berceo, the man, is relatively little and is based on what he says about himself in his works and on data that has been gleaned from the archives of the monastery of San Millán de la Cogolla.[4] He was born in the region of La Rioja in the village of Berceo. He was educated in the nearby monastery of San Millán, with which, as a secular priest and as notary for its abbot, he maintained a close association throughout his life. The monastery archives provide some biographical information on Berceo and his activities as a cleric. The records lead us to believe that he was born in the final years of the twelfth century: he was a deacon (*diácono*) in 1221, a title which carried a minimum age requirement of twenty-five. It is possible that between 1223 and 1236 Berceo studied at the Estudio General de Palencia, mentioned above.[5] In 1237, he held the rank of priest; he was still alive in 1246. The last documented reference to him by a contemporary was in 1264, when he was mentioned as having been named confessor and an executor in the will of García Gil Vañoz (ca. 1236-42; Keller *Gonzalo de Berceo* 23; Dutton *Obras* 2:34-35). Although the exact year of his death is not known, he is thought to have lived to see old age, for in his *Vida de Santa Oria* (*Life of St. Aurea*), he states that he is writing in his old age (*vegez*). The generally accepted time frame for his death is sometime after 1252 and before 1264 (Gerli *Milagros* 12; Dutton *Obras* 3:3-4).

The twelve works attributed to Berceo fall into four categories, all religiously oriented:

1. Poems of Marian devotion—*Milagros de Nuestra Señora* (*Miracles of Our Lady*), *Loores de Nuestra Señora* (*Praises of Our Lady*), and *El duelo de la Virgen* (*The Virgin's Sorrow*)

2. Saints' lives—*Vida de Santo Domingo de Silos* (*Life of St. Dominic of Silos*), *Vida de San Millán de la Cogolla* (*Life of St. Emilian, the Cowled*), *Vida de Santa Oria* (*Life of St. Aurea*), and *El martirio de San Lorenzo* (*The Martyrdom of St. Lawrence*)
3. Doctrinal poems—*El sacrificio de la Misa* (*The Sacrifice of the Mass*), and *Los signos del Juicio Final* (*The Signs that Will Appear before Judgment Day*)
4. Three short hymns (translated from known Latin originals)— "Veni Creator Spiritus, pleno de dulcedumne" (Come, Holy Spirit, Full of Sweetness), "Ave Sancta María, estrella de la mar" (Hail, Holy Mary, Star of the Sea), and "Tú Christe qe luz eres, qe alumnas el día" (Thou Christ Who Art Light that Brightens the Day)

The most important of these works are the saints' lives and *Miracles of Our Lady*. They, like all of Berceo's works, are taken from Latin sources. Because their subject matter is not original and because of the precise regularity of *cuaderna vía*, these works previously received harsh treatment by scholars who focused on their lack of originality and the repetitiveness inherent in the versification. Representative of an earlier, but certainly not universal, twentieth-century view of Berceo's works, George Tyler Northup wrote: "Here and there in the midst of dreary stretches one encounters an unexpected bit of genuine poetry. He occasionally exhibits a fine feeling for nature. But his merit is slight. He interests the philologer primarily, the student of literature only moderately" (61).[6] Despite such extreme positions as this, the majority of scholars who deal with medieval Spanish literature have maintained a keen interest in Berceo and the world he represents as well as the one he presents. Throughout the second half of the twentieth century, interest in him has continued to increase and it becomes more and more obvious that characterizations such as Northup's are inaccurate and unjustified.

As to the question of originality, one must remember, on the one hand, that in the Middle Ages a writer was not expected to be original and, on the other, that Berceo's works are not, even by modern standards, servile translations, though he may not venture far from his source material. An artistic process of selection, creation, and elaboration is at work. For example, Keller, in his discussion of Berceo's *Miracles*, says:

No matter where one chooses to make a comparison between the Latin and the Spanish rendition of it, he finds that Berceo develops surprising tones of originality. Berceo is no mere translator, as some have averred, but actually a skilled poet who reads his source knowledgeably, and then writes its content in his own words, shifting from the bare prose account of the Latin into a polished poetic version. No one can translate from prose into a strictly poetic formula like the *cuaderna vía* and expect to be literal, of course, for the demands of versification inevitably force the poet to give parallel but not exact meanings and may, indeed, compel him to wander from the exact meaning of this source. [Keller *Gonzalo de Berceo* 45]

While his works have all along been valued for their richness in language and imagery and for their popular flavor, the poet in more recent years has been shown to be a much more complicated figure than previously thought. Brian Dutton is perhaps the one scholar who has done most to advance Berceo studies during the second half of the twentieth century. He has edited Berceo's complete works[7] and undertaken a reevaluation of the poet's circumstances and, consequently, of his art. Dutton has shown that Berceo's *Vida de San Millán de la Cogolla* was written as part of a propaganda effort to spread the fame of the monastery's patron saint and to contribute to its economic prosperity during a period of serious economic decline. The most revealing aspect of this work as a propagandistic enterprise is that it figures in with a series of documentary falsifications designed to enrich the monastery.[8] The work's message depends particularly on the false privilege purported to have been granted the monastery when it was founded by Fernán González in the tenth century, but actually written by one Fernando, a contemporary of Berceo. The *Votos de San Millán*, upon which the claim was based, contained forgeries wrought by this Fernando. Thus, we have a situation in which Berceo probably knowingly participated in the diffusion of false information for the greater good of the monastery. According to the privilege, the monastery was to receive an annual sum from all the towns in Castile and parts of Navarre and would gain in prestige as well as monetarily by the enforcement of the privilege as law. While this does not mean Berceo is any less devoted to God or to the saints whose legends he tells, it does give him a pragmatic dimension and casts a new light on his motives in writing all of the works. In the case of the *Miracles of Our Lady*, for example, Dutton has shown that there existed a strong devotion to the Virgin Mary in San Millán de la Cogolla and that, in fact, the lower monastery's altar dedicated to the Virgin was the one that held the relics of Saint Millán. This altar was the object of pilgrimage and, in a time of waning interest compounded by economic difficulties, works like Berceo's *Vida de San Millán* and the *Miracles* could have contributed significantly to the monastery's popularity as a pilgrimage destination in its own right or as a secondary, but still important, point for pilgrims making their way to Santiago de Compostela. Indeed, Michael Gerli says that Berceo is "perhaps thirteenth-century Spain's most skilled and effective propagandist" ("Poet and Pilgrim" 140).

Miracles of Our Lady

Miracles of Our Lady, Berceo's most studied work, is a collection of twenty-five miracles of the Virgin Mary which are preceded by an allegorical Introduction. The form of these miracle tales, though they vary in length, is simple, as is Berceo's style in general. There is a discernible, basic pattern in the presentation, which varies somewhat according to the particular situation. Keller describes it as follows:

> [T]he poet lays the scene, giving the name of the city and the name of the protagonist. He then describes the protagonist and acquaints us with his qualities. . . . Those of evil intent receive graphic treatment also. . . . If some evil antagonist is a character, he . . . is presented early by the poet. . . . After such introductory scenes and characterizations, the miracle runs its course, ending almost invariably with one or more quatrains which relate the reward for piety and devotion or the punishment for sin and a reminder that the Virgin is a constant protectress. [*Gonzalo de Berceo* 60-62]

Wilkins offers an outline that focuses on the "dramatic form" of Berceo's miracle-tale structure:

> The typical scenario of the *Milagros*, based on the original Latin, pits the Virgin Mary, the protagonist, against the opposing force, the devil and his cohorts. A secondary character involved in the conflict is usually a faithful Christian follower of the Virgin who has erred and yet, eventually and miracu-

lously, is saved because of repentance, or, more often, some saving grace or redeeming feature which the sinner possesses. We can subdivide the plot of each miracle as follows: the beginning: point of attack, exposition; the middle: rising action, crisis, falling action; and the end: the resolution. Aside from some tragic situations in the rising action and those of a few secondary characters, the *Milagros* do not have catastrophes or tragic outcomes, and, for that reason, we can describe the end of the plot in terms of its successful resolution. The third-person narrative and direct discourse are so firmly blended in the *Milagros* that the resultant dramatic form is far removed from the Latin prose versions. [310]

The *Miracles of Our Lady* is but one example of the extensive literature of miracles of the Holy Mother which had great currency during the Middle Ages. Among these are *Miracles de Notre-Dame de Roc-Amadour* (*Miracles of Our Lady of Rocamadour*, twelfth century) and the *Miracles de la Sainte Vierge* (*Miracles of the Holy Virgin*) of Gautier de Coincy (1177-1236) in France, and the *Cantigas de Santa María* (*Canticles of Holy Mary*) of Alfonso X the Wise (1221-84) in Spain. Other more general works in this category are the *Speculum Historiale* (*Mirror of History*) of Vincent de Beauvais and the *Legenda Aurea* (*Golden Legend*) of Jacobus de Voragine. Because of similarities in presentation of the *Miracles* of Gautier de Coincy and of Berceo's own *Miracles*, it was once thought that the latter might have based his work on that of the former (See Boudet).[9] However, Richard Becker in 1910 brought to light a Latin collection (MS Thott 128) found in the Library of Copenhagen which most likely served at least indirectly as model for both Berceo and Gautier. This collection contains all of Berceo's miracles except "The Robbed Church"; moreover, the miracles in common appear in the same order in both collections.[10] "The Robbed Church" is perhaps taken from Spanish oral tradition since it deals with a Spanish subject. It should be noted that Kinkade in 1971 proposed another Latin manuscript (MS 110 of the Spanish National Library) as a more direct source for the *Miracles*.

The allegorical Introduction is the most famous and most highly praised part of Berceo's creation. Its precise source, assuming that it like his other works is not original to Berceo, remains a mystery.[11] The central metaphor, that the Virgin Mary is a perpetually green meadow where the pilgrim can rest and enjoy spiritual delights, is an elaboration of the often described *locus amoenus*, or pleasance, of the Middle Ages. Here the pleasance serves as an allegorical setting that frames and sets into perspective the twenty-five miracle tales of the Virgin's miraculous intercession. While in most of the tales she intervenes in some way on behalf of her devotees, she is also quick to punish the incorrigible or those who have offended her so severely that they are beyond redemption.

The Virgin Mary in Typological Exegesis

From the beginnings of Christianity, the teachings of the church have stressed that the coming of Christ represents the fulfillment of the Old Testament law. The Gospels themselves in their presentation of the genealogy of Christ, his words, and his deeds, deliberately underscore the concept of fulfillment as verification of his messianic claim. In the Sermon on the Mount, for example, Christ says: "Think not that I am come to destroy the law, or the prophets, I am not come to destroy, but to fulfill" (Matthew 5.17).

With the growth of the cult of the Virgin Mary, the mother of Christ also comes to serve as a figure of prophetic fulfillment. Knowledge of the Virgin Mary and her role in the fulfillment, in so far as the Gospels are concerned, comes primarily from the books of Matthew and Luke. In her book, *Alone of All Her Sex*, Warner reviews the pertinent Gospel references and their associations (1-24). Most obvious in Matthew (1.22-23) is the reference to the conception of the child Jesus by the Holy Spirit as fulfillment of the prophecy of Isaiah: "A virgin shall be with child and shall bring forth a son" (Isaiah 7.14). While Luke's narrative also contains overt allusions to the fulfillment of prophecy such as this, his is a more sophisticated, suggestive presentation that evokes many Old Testament words and events by echoing similar language without actual reference to the prophecy itself. For example, the angel Gabriel's appearances to Mary and to Zacharias, the father of John the Baptist, echo the appearance of Gabriel to the Old Testament Daniel (Daniel 9.21) who had prophesied the coming of the messiah. Gabriel tells Daniel, "thou art greatly beloved" (Daniel 9.23), just as he says to Mary, "Hail, thou that art highly favored" (Luke 1.28). Gabriel says to Mary, "Fear not, Mary, for thou hast found favor with God" and to Zacharias, "Fear not, Zacharias: for thy prayer is heard." An unidentified angel says to Daniel in the Old Testament, "Fear not, Daniel," and Daniel is subsequently struck dumb (Daniel 10.15) just as Zacharias is in the New Testament (Luke 1.20).

Despite such allusions and suggestions of prophecy, Mary is of relatively little significance in the Gospels, playing a minor role except in the two nativity narratives. However, in Christian tradition Mary is elevated to the Virgin Mother of God and Queen of Heaven. Devotion to her becomes universal in the West by the eighth century and has reached its height by Berceo's lifetime, in the thirteenth century. This devotion is nurtured in the monasteries to the point that it pervades almost all aspects of Christian thought, and the Virgin Mary begins to overshadow Christ as a revered figure. F. J. E. Raby says: "It might seem almost true to say that, in the later Middle Ages, the central object of the popular cult was in actual fact the Virgin Mary . . . invested with all those human and tender attributes in which the early Church had first clothed the figure of the Savior" (365).

Thinkers like Justin Martyr and Irenaeus in the second century perceive Mary as the second Eve, just as Christ was seen by Paul as the second Adam in 1 Corinthians 15.22 and Romans 5.14 (Warner 59). Justin Martyr says that Christ "is born of the Virgin, in order that the disobedience caused by the serpent might be destroyed in the same manner in which it had originated. For Eve, an undefiled virgin, conceived the word of the serpent, and brought forth disobedience and death. But the Virgin Mary, filled with faith and joy . . . gave birth to him . . . by whom God destroys both the serpent and those who have become like the serpent, but frees from death those who repent of their sins and believe in Christ" (quoted in Ashe 125).

The symbolism of the new Eve signals the break with the old law. Later thinkers like Origen and the Alexandrian school of exegetes in the third century look for symbols in the Old Testament that show God's plan for the new order by pointing to the messiah born of the virgin mother (Warner 61-62).

Ashe points out that in the fourth century Gregory of Nyssa extends to Mary treatment previously reserved for Christ alone— the seeking of Old Testament texts that prefigure or prophesy her. For example, Gregory says that the burning bush seen by Moses prefigures Mary. The bush was the place of divine manifestation and burned without being consumed. Similarly, Mary's womb was the receptacle for the presentation of the divine made flesh, yet her virginity remained intact (Ashe 175).

Berceo's poetry in general reflects the importance of this widespread and ever-growing devotion to the Virgin Mary. Three of his major poems—*Miracles of Our Lady, Loores de Nuestra Señora,* and *El duelo de la Virgen*—and one of his hymns ("Ave Sancta María, estrella de la mar") are devoted to her, and she is of signal importance, though by no means the central figure, in the *Vida de Santa Oria.* In two of the works, the *Loores* and the *Miracles* (specifically, the Introduction to the *Miracles*), Berceo devotes concentrated attention to the evocation of the Virgin's role in the fulfillment of the law and prophecy of the Old Testament.

Berceo's *Loores de Nuestra Señora* is one of many medieval poems written in praise of the Virgin. Berceo devotes the majority of its 233 quatrains to important events in Judeo-Christian history, from Adam and Eve up to the Crucifixion and Pentecost, and, hence, to the glorification of our Lady as protectress of the faithful. Close examination shows that Berceo's insistence on Old Testament events and figures reflects (with particular emphasis on the role of Christ's mother) the generally held view that the Old Testament was fulfilled by the coming of the New Testament messiah in what Warner has referred to as "one unbroken chain of prophecy" (62).

Obviously written within this same tradition, the Introduction to Berceo's *Miracles* represents a compact but evocative narration which is followed by a gloss containing many of the same images of prophetic and typological fulfillment found in the *Loores.* The allegorical Introduction is the portion of Berceo's work richest in imagery and symbolism. Berceo opens the poem with a quatrain of exhortation to his audience. He names himself as a pilgrim in the second quatrain, and the allegorical narrative begins. The narrative proper ends with a comparison of the meadow to paradise in quatrains 14 and 15. This comparison is not casually made; the correspondence Virgin-meadow-paradise is the key to the allegory and to the meaning of the *Miracles* as a whole. The Virgin is linked symbolically to the Garden of Eden, the earthly paradise lost, and the fall of mankind. Her part in the salvation of mankind, as the second Eve, is Berceo's central theme. Just as God in his infinite goodness created Eden, so has he created this second garden paradise, this second Eve—Mary— who leads humankind to the third and heavenly paradise.

Quatrain 15 continues with imagery of the Fall and evokes the whole history of humankind in the Christian framework, suggesting that the meadow (Mary) undoes the sin of Adam and Eve:

> The fruit of the trees was sweet and delicious;
> if Adam had eaten such fruit,
> he would not have been so badly deceived.
> Neither Eve nor her husband would have suffered such harm!

With quatrain 16, Berceo expresses metaphorically his desire to take the husk off the allegory in order to expose its underlying meaning. He begins the gloss, explaining the significance of the various aspects of the narrative and the attributes of the garden. For example, the birds of the meadow represent all those who sang the virtues of our Lady—including the prophets (like Isaiah) and the patriarchs. Then, in quatrains 31-41, he arrives at an extensive series of allusions to the Virgin as fulfillment of prophecy. In quatrain 31, he explains the flowers of the meadow as representing the names or titles of the Blessed Virgin. And in quatrains 33-41, he lists these names, giving varying degrees of explanation, but none so complete as those found in the first section of the *Loores*.

The following titles are bestowed upon the Blessed Virgin because they have been interpreted as prophetic of her or have been applied to her through typological exegesis: fleece of Gideon (34a); sling of David (34c); fountain (35a); closed gate (36a); Zion (37a); throne of Solomon (37c); vine, grape, almond, pomegranate (39a); olive, cedar, balsam, palm (39c); staff of Moses (40a); rod of Aaron (41ab).

The Fleece of Gideon is considered a prefigurement of the virginity of the Blessed Mother and is one of the best known of such symbols (Raby 371). The sling of David in the well-known story of David and Goliath (1 Samuel 17) prefigures her in that she launched the stone, her son, into the world to strike down evil and bring salvation.

The fountain is possibly the sealed fountain of the Song of Solomon: "A garden enclosed is my sister, my spouse; a spring shut up, a fountain sealed" (Song of Solomon 4.12) which was considered a prefigurement of her virginal womb. This idea of her unblemished virginity is also behind the interpretation of the closed gate of Ezekiel (Ezekiel 44.1-3) which is seen in Loores, and the image of the "closed gate" appears here again in Berceo's words: "She is called the Closed Gate; / for us She is open, to give us entrance" (*Miracles* 36a).

She is Zion (37a), or the virgin daughter of Zion, evoked in so many Old Testament passages such as "Sing and rejoice, O daughter of Zion: for, lo, I come, and I will dwell in the midst of thee, saith the Lord." As the throne of Solomon (37c) described in 1 Kings 10.18-20, the Virgin is unique in beauty and virtue, for "there was not the like made in any kingdom." The gold of the throne symbolizes her charity, the ivory her chastity. The association with Solomon also associates her with wisdom and justice.

In quatrain 39, she is vine, grape, almond, pomegranate, olive, cedar, balsam and palm. These images are consistent with the enclosed garden of the Song of Solomon (4.12), which holds among other things an orchard; however, they seem more specifically to relate to the twenty-fourth chapter of the apocryphal Book of Ecclesiasticus, in which the female figure Wisdom says:

> I grew tall like a cedar in Lebanon . . .
> I grew tall like a palm tree in En-gedi . . .
> like a beautiful olive tree in the field . . .
> like a vine I caused loveliness to bud,
> and my blossoms became glorious and abundant fruits.
> [Ecclesiasticus 24.13-17]

Both of these passages were applied typologically to the Virgin Mary.

The last two names are Staff of Moses and Rod of Aaron. The staff of Moses, Berceo says, confounded the sorcerers of Pharaoh and opened the waters of the sea for the children of Israel but closed them on the pursuing Egyptians (Exodus 14.21-27). Because the staff was significant in the salvation of Israel and acted contrary to the laws of nature, particularly when it spontaneously turned into a serpent, it was seen as a prefigurement of the virginal conception of Christ in Mary (Warner 62). A similar interpretation was applied to the rod of Aaron, the last of Mary's names mentioned by Berceo in the Introduction to the *Miracles* and used also in the *Loores*. God caused Aaron's rod to bloom and produce almonds as a sign that Aaron was chosen and that the Israelites should not continue to resist his leadership (Numbers 17.1-8).

It is clear from the *Loores* and the Introduction to the *Miracles* that the figures which Berceo gives as prophetic prefigurations of the role of the Virgin serve to elevate her to a level of importance in human salvation very near, if not equal, to that of Christ.

While Mary's elevated position may not adhere to strict Catholic theology, neither is it a strange aberration that makes Berceo's perception of her role unique. Rather, his perception of her role is formed by a centuries-old tradition that found its fullest flowering in the writings of Saint Bernard in the twelfth century. Furthermore, Berceo's insistence on prophetic fulfillment links his work to the long chain of previous writers and serves artistically as one element of unity in the works. Prophecy is of particular significance as a unifying motif within Berceo's Marian works and sets them and their audience within the continuum that leads to salvation.

The *Miracles* within the Context of Pilgrimage

In the ninth century, the tomb of the Apostle Saint James the Greater (Santiago to the Spanish), was found in Galicia in northwestern Spain and the shrine there established became the goal of the famous pilgrimage to Santiago de Compostela.[12] The impact of the pilgrim route crossing northern Spain from the Pyrenees to Galicia was not only religious but also economic, cultural, and political. Pilgrimages to Santiago were particularly promoted during the eleventh century by King Sancho el Mayor of Navarre. The Cluniac order established itself along the route and provided lodging for the travellers. Since this was a French order, the trans-Pyrenees connections were an important force in bringing new ideas from the rest of Europe, especially France, into the Iberian Peninsula. The monasteries themselves vied for pilgrims and even those not on the direct pilgrim route served as lesser destinations or side trips for pilgrims. Michael Gerli points out that in the eleventh century the Monastery of San Millán de la Cogolla (Berceo's monastery), had acquired the pilgrim hostel of Azofra near Nájera on the Santiago route. Pilgrims who stopped there were no doubt encouraged to make the excursion to San Millán to pray in the Sanctuary of the Virgin Mary. Gerli believes that Berceo's *Miracles* were probably read or recited in Azofra in order to entertain pilgrims and, perhaps more importantly, to entice them to go to San Millán to pay homage to the Blessed Mother (Gerli *Milagros* 23). Be that as it may, San Millán was known to attract pilgrims in its own right, as many came to pay homage to Saint Millán or to the Virgin, whose cult was firmly established there.

The reader of Berceo's *Miracles* will note not only the importance of the concept of pilgrimage in the work but also the orality of the text. The fact that the work was written to be read or recited and even acted out for an audience of religious pilgrims explains to a large degree both the motivation for the work's composition as well as the nature of its presentation. With his analysis of the "dramatic design" of the *Miracles*, Wilkins raises the possibility of the work as an antecedent of Spanish drama. Other scholars have gone a step further, suggesting that works such as the *Miracles* actually were acted out through mime while a reader (possibly the poet himself) read or recited the narration. This view, by placing the *Miracles* and other *clerecía* works within the tradition of dramatic art, helps to fill in the three-century gap in the early development of Castilian "drama."[13]

Gerli has shown that the inscribed audience of the *Miracles* is in fact an audience of pilgrims for whom the work's language, discourse, and imagery are specifically tailored. The central human figure in the allegorical introduction is the narrator who presents himself as a pilgrim, a strategem by which the poet-narrator immediately identifies himself with his audience and gains their confidence as well as their interest. Moreover, two of the miracle tales have pilgrims as their human protagonists: "The Pilgrim Deceived by the Devil" and "The Shipwrecked Pilgrim Saved by the Virgin."

The Translation

Considering the importance accorded Berceo's *Miracles*, it is surprising that it has not previously been translated into English. This can be explained in part by the fact that the work was not generally known in Spain until the eighteenth century, when Tomás Antonio Sánchez rediscovered and published Berceo's works. While the work's importance as one of the monuments of medieval Spanish literature is firmly established, the difficulties of translating the *Miracles*, with its stringent versification pattern and Latinized syntax, may have daunted many who might have considered undertaking the project. The present translation was done with no attempt to adapt the work to English rhyme and meter. The foremost consideration was to present in English a readable translation that would preserve the meaning and something of the flavor of the original, including its orality. In order to accomplish this, the translators have maintained the strophe divisions so that each strophe in English is a faithful and readable translation of the corresponding strophe in the original. Where English grammar and syntax allow, the sense of each line of verse and even of each hemistich has also been preserved. Occasionally, of course, the exigencies of English have required the rearrangement of some of the lines within a strophe. While there has been no attempt at casting Berceo's Spanish into the language of his English contemporaries, the translators have aimed to create through vocabulary, syntax, style, and reverential capitalization the feeling in modern readers that Berceo is speaking to them from a world in which the Virgin Mary was a vital presence in the lives of Christian believers—a world in which the written word was revered and its message was to be shared among those of kindred spirit.

The translation is based on Brian Dutton's critical edition of the *Miracles*, but the translators have found invaluable the work of other editors, namely Michael Gerli, Vicente Beltrán, Daniel Devoto, and Antonio G. Solalinde.[14] Dutton's reordering of strophes, primarily the reversal in the order of Miracles 24 and 25, has been followed, with dual numbering of those strophes affected. The work of the translation itself has been done in the spirit of true collaboration. Each translator took initial responsibility for approximately one half (in terms of lines of verse) of the total volume of the work. As initial translations were completed, work was exchanged and corrections and revisions were suggested and made. Changes have continued to be made for the sake of accuracy and style up until the time of publication. Terry Mount has written the introduction to the translation in order to orient the reader to the historical and literary context of the *Miracles*; Annette Cash has compiled the extensive bibliography which follows the translated text. This bibliography, divided into two parts, gives editions of the *Miracles* in Spanish as well as critical studies of the work and will prove to be an invaluable resource for readers who desire further to explore the depth and breadth of Berceo's remarkable miracle collection.

Notes

1. See, for example, Menéndez Pidal, 337.
2. *Romance* refers to Romance language, in this case Old Spanish.

Romance was used to refer to the vernacular languages derived from the language of the Romans, i.e., Latin.

3. See Nelson's study and edition of the *Alexandre*.

4. See Dutton, "The Profession of Gonzalo de Berceo and the Paris Manuscript of the *Libro de Alexandre*"; "Gonzalo de Berceo: unos datos biográficos"; and "La fecha del nacimiento de Gonzalo de Berceo."

5. This would explain his vast learning, the title of *maestro* (master) that he uses with his name in *Miracles*, strophe 2, and his reference to Tello Téllez de Meneses, Bishop of Palencia and founder of the Estudio General, in *Miracles*, strophe 325. The title *maestro*, however, may refer, instead, to Berceo's status as a priest or "master of confession," as critics prior to Dutton understood the term, basing their interpretation on *Miracles* 492a. See Dutton, *Obras* 2:34-35.

6. C.R. Post, *Medieval Spanish Allegory* (Cambridge: Harvard University Press, 1915) 136, is also disdainful of Berceo and his manner, which he assumes to be unoriginal and decidedly borrowed from the French.

7. Brian Dutton, ed., *Obras completas* by Gonzalo de Berceo, 5 vols. (London: Támesis Books, 1967-1981). Volume 1 was published with the title *La vida de San Millán de la Cogolla*. Volume 2 is the edition of the *Milagros de Nuestra Señora*.

8. The texts and details are included in Dutton's edition of *La vida de San Millán de la Cogolla* (*Obras* vol. 1). For a summary in English, see Keller *Gonzalo de Berceo* 68-70.

9. For a description in English of some of the problems of the sources of the *Milagros*, see Keller *Gonzalo de Berceo* 44-50. See also Dutton *Obras* 2:13-14, and the commentaries following each miracle tale.

10. Dutton reverses the "traditional" order of the last two miracle tales in his critical edition so that "The Robbed Church" is the twenty-fourth and "The Miracle of Theophilus" is the twenty-fifth miracle. We have followed this as well as other such suggestions of his for reordering quatrains. (See Dutton, ed., *Milagros*, 17.)

11. For a thorough presentation on the sources of the Introduction, see Dutton, *Obras* 2:36-45.

12. Still today thousands of pilgrims, whether by bus, auto, bicycle, or on foot, follow the traditional route to visit the shrine of Spain's patron saint in Santiago de Compostela. Many, as in Berceo's day, take side trips to the monastaries of San Millán and Santo Domingo de Silos. For an account of the modern-day experience, see Stanton.

13. See especially Gerli, "Poet and Pilgrim," and Richard P. Kinkade, "Sermon in the Round." Kinkade offers his study as a plau-

sible explanation for the apparent lacuna between the twelfth-century *Auto de los Reyes Magos* (*Play of the Three Wise Men*, the earliest extant religious play in any vernacular) and the fifteenth-century *Representación del nacimiento de Nuestro Señor* (*Representation of the Nativity of Our Lord*) by Gómez Manrique. Further discussion of manifestations of dramatic "staging" techniques in Spain in the thirteenth century, especially as related to the *Canticles of Holy Mary* of Alfonso the Wise, can be found in Keller and Kinkade (16-17) and in Keller, "Drama, Ritual, and Incipient Opera." 14. As the work on the translation nears completion, we note the appearance of another edition of Berceo's works by Dutton: *Obra Completa*, ed. Brian Dutton et al. (Madrid: Espasa-Calpe, 1992?).

Works Cited

Ashe, Geoffrey. *The Virgin*. London: Routledge and Kegan Paul, 1976.

Becker, Richard. *Gonzalo de Berceo. "Los Milagros" und ihre Grundlagen*. Strassburg: Universitäts Bruchdruckerei, 1910.

Beltrán, Vicente, ed. *Milagros de Nuestra Señora*, by Gonzalo de Berceo. 3d ed. Barcelona: Planeta, 1990.

Boudet, Théodore Joseph. *Les vieux auteurs castillans*. Paris: Didier, 1861-62.

Devoto, Daniel, ed. *Milagros de Nuestra Señora*, by Gonzalo de Berceo. Odres Nuevos. Madrid: Castalia, 1969. Modernized version.

Dutton, Brian. "La fecha del nacimiento de Gonzalo de Berceo." *Berceo* 94-95 (1978): 265-68.

———. "Gonzalo de Berceo: unos datos biográficos." In *Actas del Primer Congreso Internacional de Hispanistas*, ed. Frank Pierce and Cyril A. Jones. Oxford: Dolphin, 1964. 249-54.

———, ed. *Obras completas*, by Gonzalo de Berceo. 5 vols. London: Támesis, 1967-81. (Vol. 1 published as *La vida de San Millán de la Cogolla*.)

———. "The Profession of Gonzalo de Berceo and the Paris Manuscript of the *Libro de Alexandre*." *Bulletin of Hispanic Studies* 37 (1960): 137-45.

Gerli, Michael, ed. *Milagros de Nuestra Señora*, 4th ed., by Gonzalo de Berceo. Madrid: Cátedra, 1989.

———. "Poet and Pilgrim: Discourse, Language, Imagery, and Audience in Berceo's *Milagros de Nuestra Señora*." In *Hispanic Medieval Studies in Honor of Samuel G. Armistead*, ed. E. Michael Gerli and Harvey L. Sharrer. Madison: Hispanic Seminary of Medieval Studies, 1992. 140-51.

Keller, John Esten. "Drama, Ritual, and Incipient Opera in Alfonso's *Cantigas*." In *Emperor of Culture: Alfonso X the Learned of*

Castile and His Thirteenth-Century Renaissance, ed. Robert I. Burns. Philadelphia: University of Pennsylvania Press, 1990. 72-89.

———. *Gonzalo de Berceo.* Twayne's World Authors Series. 187. New York: Twayne, 1972.

Keller, John Esten, and Richard P. Kinkade. *Iconography in Medieval Spanish Literature.* Lexington: Univeristy Press of Kentucky, 1984.

Kinkade, Richard P. "A New Latin Source for Berceo's *Milagros*: MS110 of Madrid's Biblioteca Nacional." *Romance Philology* 25 (1971): 188-92.

———. "Sermon in the Round: The *Mester de Clerecía* as Dramatic Art." In *Studies in Honor of Gustavo Correa,* ed. Charles B. Faulhaber, Richard P. Kinkade, and T. A. Perry. Potomac, Md.: Scripta Humanistica, 1986. 127-36.

Menéndez Pidal, Ramón. *Poesía juglaresca y orígenes de las literaturas románicas.* Madrid: Instituto de Estudios Políticos, 1957.

Nelson, Dana. *Gonzalo de Berceo: "El libro de Alexandre."* *Reconstrucción crítica.* Madrid: Gredos, 1979.

Northup, George Tyler. *An Introduction to Spanish Literature,* 3d ed. rev., ed. Nicholson B. Adams. Chicago: University of Chicago Press, 1960.

Orduña, Germán, ed. *Vida de Santo Domingo de Silos,* by Gonzalo de Berceo. Salamanca: Anaya, 1968.

Post, C.R. *Medieval Spanish Allegory.* Cambridge: Harvard University Press, 1915.

Raby, F.J.E. *A History of Christian-Latin Poetry from the Beginnings to the Close of the Middle Ages,* 2d ed. Oxford: Oxford University Press, 1966.

Rico, Francisco. "La clerecía del mester." *Hispanic Review* 53 (1985) 1-23, 127-50.

Sánchez, Tomás Antonio. *Colección de poesías castellanas anteriores al siglo XV,* vol. 2. Madrid: A. de Sancha, 1779-90.

Smith, Colin, ed. *Poema de mio Cid.* Madrid: Cátedra, 1977.

Solalinde, Antonio [García]. *Milagros de Nuestra Señora,* 5th ed. Clásicos Castellanos 44. Madrid: Espasa-Calpe, 1958.

Stanton, Edward. *Road of Stars to Santiago.* Lexington: University Press of Kentucky, 1994.

Uria Maqua, Isabela. "Sobre la unidad del mester de clerecía del siglo XIII. Hacia un replanteamiento de la cuestión." In *Actas de las III Jornadas Berceanas,* ed. Claudio García Turza. Logroño: Instituto de Estudios Riojanos, 1981. 179-88.

Warner, Marina. *Alone of All Her Sex.* New York: Knopf, 1976.

Wilkins, Heanon. "Dramatic Design in Berceo's *Milagros de Nuestra Señora.*" In *Hispanic Studies in Honor of Alan D. Deyermond: A North American Tribute,* ed. John S. Miletich. Madison, Wis.: Hispanic Seminary of Medieval Studies, 1986. 309-24.

❖ MIRACLES OF OUR LADY

Introduction

1   Friends and vassals of Almighty God,
if it pleases you to listen to me,
I would like to relate a fortunate experience.
Afterwards you will truly consider it wonderful.

2   I, Master Gonzalo de Berceo,
while on a pilgrimage happened to pause in a meadow[1]
green and untouched, full of flowers—
a desirable place for a weary man.

3   The flowers there emitted a marvelous fragrance;
they were refreshing to the spirit and to the body.
From each corner sprang clear, flowing fountains,
very cool in summer and warm in winter.

4   There was a profusion of fine trees—
pomegranate and fig, pear and apple,
and many other fruits of various kinds.
But none were spoiled or sour.

5   The greenness of the meadow, the fragrance of the
       flowers,
the shade of the trees of soothing aromas
refreshed me completely and I ceased to perspire.
Anyone could live with those fragrances.

6   Never in this world did I find so delightful a place,
nor so soothing a shade, nor so pleasant a fragrance;
I removed my garment for a more comfortable repose
and lay under the shade of a beautiful tree.

---

1. The meadow is an evocation of the medieval *locus amoenus* and symbolically associates the garden paradise with the Virgin Mary. As the allegory of the meadow unfolds, emphasis is placed on its perfection and perpetually pure or virginal state.

7 Lying in the shade, I forgot all my cares;
  I heard sweet, modulated bird songs.
  There never was heard music of organs so finely tuned,
  nor could more harmonious sounds be made.

8 Some birds carried the fifth, while others doubled,
  others held the basic melody, keeping everyone from
    erring.
  Upon resting and moving, they all waited for each other.
  No dull or raucous birds came near there!

9 There was no organist, *vihuela* player,
  nor *giga*, psaltery, or *rota*-player's hand,[2]
  nor other instrument, or tongue, or so clear a voice
  whose song would be worth a penny[3] in comparison.

10 Although we told you of all these virtues,
  rest assured we did not tell a tenth of them
  for there was such diversity of splendors
  that neither priors nor abbots could count them.

11 The meadow I am telling you about had another fine
    quality:
  in neither heat nor cold did it lose its beauty;
  it was always green in its entirety.
  It did not lose its verdure in any storm.

12 As soon as I had stretched out on the ground,
  I was immediately freed of all suffering;
  I forgot all worries and past burdens.
  Anyone living there would be very lucky indeed!

13 No matter how many men or birds came there
  and carried away all the flowers they wished,
  there was never a lack of flowers in the meadow;
  for each one that they plucked three and four would
    spring up.[4]

---

2. The *vihuela*, the *giga*, and the *rota* are medieval stringed instruments. The *vihuela* is similar to the guitar. The *giga* is a kind of viola and the *rota* a kind of harp.

3. *Dinero*, a coin of small value; therefore, the translation "penny" seems appropriate here and in strophe 324d.

4. The spontaneous regeneration described here is in keeping with the "intactness" of the meadow mentioned in quatrains 2 and 11.

14   This meadow seemed like Paradise
into which God put such great grace, such great blessing.
He who created such a thing was a wise master;
any man who should dwell here would never lose his
    sight.

15   The fruit of the trees was sweet and delicious;
if Adam had eaten such fruit,
he would not have been so badly deceived.
Neither Eve nor her husband would have suffered
    such harm!

16   Gentle people and friends, what we have just said
is an obscure parable and we wish to explain it.
Let us remove the husk and get into the marrow.[5]
Let us take what is within, and what is without let us
    leave aside.

17   All we who live and stand upright,[6]
even if we are in prison or bedridden,
are pilgrims walking down the road.
Saint Peter says so—we prove it to you through him.

·18   As long as we live here, we dwell in a foreign land;
the everlasting dwelling place we await on high.
Our pilgrimage, then, we finish
when we send our souls to Paradise.

19   On this pilgrimage we have a good meadow
in which any weary pilgrim will find refuge:
the Glorious Virgin, Mother of the Good Servant,
the equal of Whom has never been found.

20   This meadow was always green in purity
for Her virginity never was stained;
post partum et in partu[7] She truly was a virgin
undefiled, incorrupt in Her integrity.

---

5. The metaphor of the husk (*corteza*) and the marrow (*meollo*) is another common medieval metaphor referring to a real or symbolic meaning beyond the surface meaning.

6. Although the manuscript reads "en piedes andamos" (walk on our feet, or upright), Dutton corrects to "en piedes estamos" (stand on our feet, or upright) to avoid repetition of the rhyming word *andamos* that occurs again in 17c.

7. Latin: "after giving birth [to Christ] and during [His] birth."

21 The four clear streams flowing from the meadow
    signified the four Gospels,
    for the Evangelists,[8] the four who delivered them,
    talked with Her as they wrote.

22 Everything they wrote, She emended.
    That which She praised was indeed true.
    It seems that She was the source from which all waters
        flowed
    while without Her nothing received guidance.

23 The shade of the trees, good, sweet and healthful,
    in which all pilgrims take respite
    indeed are the prayers that Holy Mary says,
    She who prays for sinners day and night.

24 All who are in this world, the righteous and the sinful,
    regular and secular clergy, kings and emperors,
    we all hasten there, vassals and lords,
    all of us seek Her shade to gather the flowers.

25 The trees that make sweet and blessed shade
    are the holy miracles that the Glorious One performs
    for they are much sweeter than the delicious sugar
    given to the sick in their delirious suffering.[9]

26 The birds that sing in those fruit trees,
    that have sweet voices and sing devout songs,
    they are Augustine, Gregory, and others,
    who wrote about Her true deeds.

27 These had love and loyalty for Her
    and praised Her deeds with all their might;
    they told of Her, each in his own way;
    but throughout it all they held to one belief.

28 The nightingale sings with fine skill,
    and even the lark makes great melody,
    but Isaiah sang much better,
    as did the other prophets, honored company.

29 The apostles sang in a most natural tone;

---

8. Matthew, Mark, Luke, and John (authors of the four gospels).

9. Sugar was a luxury item in the Middle Ages and used primarily in medicines.

the confessors and martyrs did likewise;
the virgins followed the great and powerful Mother
singing before Her a very joyous song.

30   In all the churches, every day,
the clergy sings lauds before Her.
All pay court to the Virgin Mary:
they are the most pleasing nightingales.

31   Let us turn to the flowers that comprise the meadow,
which make it beautiful, fair, and serene.
The flowers are the names the book gives
to the Virgin Mary, Mother of the Good Servant.[10]

32   The Blessed Virgin is called Star,
Star of the Seas, Longed-For Guide,
She is watched by mariners in peril
for when they see Her, their ship is guided.

33   She is called and She is Queen of Heaven,
Temple of Jesus Christ, Morning Star,
Natural Mistress, Merciful Neighbor,
Health and Cure of Bodies and Souls.

34   She is the Fleece that was Gideon's,
on which fell the rain, a great vision;
She is the Sling with which young David
destroyed the ferocious giant.

35   She is the Fount from which we all drink,
She gave us the food of which we all eat;
She is called the Port to which we all hasten,
and the Gate through which we all await entrance.

36   She is called the Closed Gate;
for us She is open, to give us entrance;
She is the Gall-Cleaned Dove
in Whom lies no wrath; She is always pleased.

37   She rightfully is called Zion,
for She is our Watchtower, our Defense;

---

10. These names, explained in quatrains 32-41, show the importance of the
Virgin Mary in the medieval mind and especially are indicative of the interpretation of Old Testament figures as pointing to her and her role in the
fulfillment of the divine plan. For a general explanation of their significance in typological exegesis, see our Introduction.

She is called the Throne of King Solomon,
king of justice and admirably wise.

38 There exists no goodly name
that in some way does not apply to Her;
there is none that does not have its root in Her,
neither Sancho nor Domingo, not Sancha nor Dominga.[11]

39 She is called Vine, She is Grape, Almond and
 Pomegranate,
replete with its grains of grace,[12]
Olive, Cedar, Balsam, leafy Palm,
Rod upon which the serpent was raised.

40 The Staff that Moses carried in his hand,[13]
that confounded the wise men esteemed by Pharaoh,
the one that parted the waters and then closed them—
if it did not signify the Virgin, it signified nothing.

41 If we think upon the other staff
that settled the dispute concerning Aaron,[14]
it signified nothing else—so says the text—
but the Glorious One, and with good reason.

42 Gentlefolk and friends, in vain do we argue
for we enter a great well, whose bottom we cannot find;
we would read more of Her names
than there are flowers in the largest field we know.

43 We have already said that the fruit trees
in which the birds were singing their various songs
were Her holy miracles, great and outstanding,
which we sing on the principal feast days.

44 But I want to leave behind those singing birds,
the shade, the founts, and the aforementioned flowers

---

11. Berceo uses the common names Sancho and Domingo and their femi-
nine equivalents to indicate that all Christian names in some way can be
traced to the Virgin Mary. Sancho is derived from *sanctus* (holy), and
Domingo from *dominicus* (belonging to the Lord). The use of these names
can be compared to that of the English names Tom, Dick, and Harry to
indicate any and everyone.

12. The pomegranate is notable for the countless seeds in each of its fruits.

13. Exodus 4.2-4; 4.17; 9.23; 10.13; 14.21; 14.27.

14. Numbers 17.

and about these fruit trees so full of sweetness
write a few verses, gentlefolk and friends.

45 I want to climb up into those trees for a little while
and write about some of Her miracles.
May the Glorious One guide me so that I may complete
     the task
for I would not dare to undertake it otherwise.

46 I will take it as a miracle wrought by the Glorious One
if She should deign to guide me in this task:
Mother Full of Grace, Powerful Queen,
guide me in it, for You are merciful.

The Chasuble of Saint Ildephonsus

47   In Spain I desire at once to begin:
      in the great city of Toledo, a famous place,
      for I do not know where else to begin
      because there are more miracles than the sand on the
            seashore.

48   In fair Toledo, that royal city
      which lies above the Tagus, that mighty river,
      there was an archbishop, a loyal cleric
      who was a true friend of the Glorious One.

49   According to the text,[1] they called him Ildephonsus,[2]
      a shepherd who gave his flock good pasture,
      a holy man who possessed great wisdom;
      all that we may say his deeds reveal.

50   He was always partial to the Glorious One,
      Never did man have more love for lady,
      he sought to serve Her with all his might,
      and did so sensibly and most prudently.

51   Besides his many other great services
      there are two in the writing which are most notable:
      he wrote a book of beautiful sayings about Her
      and Her virginity, contradicting three infidels.[3]

---

1. Berceo refers to a written text, his Latin source.

2. Saint Ildephonsus (606-667) became archbishop of Toledo in 657, unified the Spanish liturgy and is especially known for his devotion to the Blessed Virgin and his treatise on her perpetual virginity.

3. This is a reference to the *Libellus de virginitate Sanctae Mariae contra*

52 And the loyal cleric served Her in another way:
he changed Her feast day to the middle of December,
the one that fell in March, that most signal day
when Gabriel came with his wonderful message.

53 When Gabriel came with the message,
when sweetly he said: "Hail, Mary,"
and told her the news that She would bear the Messiah
remaining as virginal as She was on that day.

54 At that time of the year, as is well known,
the Church does not sing a song of joy[4]
and such a signal day does not get its rightful due;
if we consider it well, he did a great favor.

55 Her loyal friend did a great and prudent deed;
by placing that feast day near the Nativity,
he joined a good grape vine to a good arbor—
the Mother with the Son, a pair without equal.

56 The lenten season is a time of affliction;
no hallelujahs are sung nor are processions made;
this wise man thought about all of this—
and later because of it he earned an honorable reward.

57 Saint Ildephonsus, loyal clergyman,
prepared for the Virgin a general holy day;
there were few in Toledo who stayed in their lodgings
and did not go to Mass in the Cathedral.

58 The holy archbishop, that loyal cleric,
was prepared to begin the Mass;
he was seated on his precious throne
when the Glorious One brought him a most honorable gift.

59 The Mother of the King of Majesty appeared unto him
with a book of great brightness in Her hand;
it was the book he had written about Her virginity.[5]
Ildephonsus was very much pleased!

---

tres infideles, more synonymorum conscriptus a beato Ildefonso, Toletanae sedis episcopo, a treatise on the perpetual virginity of the Blessed Virgin Mary written by Saint Ildephonsus.

4. Berceo is referring to Lent, the penitential period before Easter, which he mentions specifically in 56ab.

5. This is the book referred to in strophe 51cd.

60   She extended to him another favor, never before heard:
She gave him a chasuble sewn without a needle;
it was an angelic work, not woven by human kind;
She spoke but few words to him, a good and perfect speech.

61   "Friend," She said, "know that I am pleased with you.
You have sought for me not single but double honor:
you wrote a good book about me and have praised me well,
you have made me a new feast day, which was not the
custom.

62   For your new Mass of this feast day,
I bring you a gift of great value:
a chasuble, a truly precious one, in which you may sing
today on the holy day of the Nativity.

63   The throne upon which you now rest
(64)⁶ is reserved for your body alone;
the vesting of this chasuble is granted to you;
anyone else who wears it will not be well regarded."

64   Having said these words, the Glorious Mother
(63) vanished from sight; he saw nothing more of Her;
the precious Person had finished Her mission,
the Mother of Christ, His Servant and Spouse.

65   This lovely feast day about which we have spoken
was soon approved by the General Council;⁷
it is observed and celebrated by many churches;
as long as this world endures, it will not be forgotten.

66   When our Heavenly Lord Jesus Christ so willed it,
Saint Ildephonsus, that precious confessor, died;
the Glorious One, Mother of the Creator, honored him;
She did great honor to his body and even greater to his
soul.

67   A foolish canon was elevated to archbishop;
he was extremely proud and light of brain—

---

6. The inversion of verses [(64)(63)] here follows Dutton, who saw that the order in the manuscript [(63)(64)] makes little sense. Other similar instances are found at strophes 248-49 and 517-19.

7. In the year 656, the Tenth Council of Toledo officially moved the Feast of the Annunciation from March 25 to December 18.

he wanted to be the equal of the other; in that, he was
    wrong.
And the people of Toledo did not consider it good.

68   He seated himself upon the throne of his predecessor
and demanded the chasuble the Creator had given him;
that foolish sinner said some crazy things
which angered the Mother of God Our Lord.

69   He said some very foolish things:
"Ildephonsus was never of greater dignity than I,
truly I am just as well consecrated as he was,
and we are all equal in our humanity!"

70   If Siagrio had not gone so far,
if he had only held his tongue a little,
he would not have fallen into the Creator's wrath
where we fear—oh, woeful sin—he is lost!

71   He ordered his ministers to bring the chasuble
so that he might go into Mass and lead the confessional
    prayer,
but he was not permitted to do so, nor did he have the
    power,
because that which God does not will to be can never be.

72   Although the holy vestment was ample in size,
on Siagrio it was exceedingly tight;
it held his throat like a hard chain,
and he was suffocated right then because of his great folly.

73   The Glorious Virgin, Star of the Sea,
knows how to reward Her friends well;
She knows how to reward the good for their goodness
and how to punish those who serve Her badly.

74   Friends, we should serve such a Mother well:
in serving Her we seek our own benefit:
we honor our bodies, we save our souls;
and for only a little service we reap great rewards.

The Fornicating Sexton

75 Friends, if you would wait a short while,
there is yet another miracle that I would like to tell,
which God deigned to reveal through Holy Mary
whose milk He suckled with His own mouth.

76 A blessed monk was in a monastery;
where it was I do not find in the reading,[1] so I cannot say.
He loved Holy Mary with all his heart
and each day genuflected before Her image.

77 Each day he bowed before Her image,
he would bend his knees and say: "Hail, Mary."
The abbot of the house gave him the sextonship
for he considered him prudent and free from folly.

78 The wicked enemy, vicar of Beelzebub,
who always was and is the enemy of good people,
that wily adversary was able to stir things up so much
that he corrupted the monk: he made him a fornicator.

79 He took up a bad habit, that crazy sinner:
at night when the abbot was in bed,
he would go out of the dormitory, through the church;
thus the lewd man hastened to his wicked work.

80 Upon leaving as well as upon returning
he would have to pass by the altar;
and so accustomed was he to genuflecting and saying the "Ave"
that not a single time did he forget it.

81 There was a goodly river running near the monastery.
The monk always had to cross it;

---

1. Berceo refers to what he reads in his source text.

once when returning from committing his folly,
he fell in and drowned, outside the abbey.

82 When the hour to sing matins[2] arrived
there was no sexton to ring the call;
all the monks got up, each from his own place,
and went to the church to awaken the friar.

83 They opened the church as best they could,
they searched for the key-keeper but could not find him.
They went everywhere looking high and low
and finally found him where he lay drowned.

84 What could this be? They had not the slightest idea
whether he had died or had been killed; they could not
  decide.
The anxiety was great and even greater the sorrow,
for the place, because of all this, would fall into disrepute.

85 While the body was lying in the river as if in a bath,[3]
let us tell of the dispute in which the soul found itself:
a great crowd of devils came for it,
to carry it off to Hell, a place devoid of all pleasure.

86 While the devils were carrying it like a ball,
the angels saw it and came down to it.
The devils then made a very strong argument:
that it did not belong to the angels and they should get
  away from it.

87 The angels had no grounds for reclaiming the soul,
since the man had met a bad end; and that was so, without
  doubt.
They could not wrest it from the devils even a little
and had to withdraw sadhearted from the fray.

88 The Glorious One, Queen of All, came to rescue the soul,
for the devils were focusing on evil alone;

---

2. One of the canonical hours sung before dawn.

3. Berceo seems to be emphasizing the separation of the body from the
spirit. Since the body is in the water, it is lying as if "in a bath" and coming
to no real harm. In fact, the evocation of the bath implies that the body is
quite content, experiencing true pleasure (see also strophes 152, 448, and
609). The real harm or unpleasantness is awaiting the soul in hell, "a place
devoid of all pleasure" (85d).

She ordered them to wait and they dared not do otherwise,
She took them to task very firmly and very well.

89 She presented an eloquent argument:
"Against this soul, you fools," She said, "you have nothing.
While it was in its body, it was my devotee;
it would be wrong for me to abandon it now."

90 The spokesman for the other side responded
(he was a wise devil, clever and very precise):
"You are Mother of the Son, the Just Judge,
who does not like force and is not pleased with it.

91 It is written that wherever a man dies,
whether in good or in evil, he is judged accordingly;
so if you break the law in this case,
you will be undermining the entire Gospel."

92 "You are speaking foolishly," said the Glorious One.
"I will not challenge you, for you are a despicable beast.
When the sexton left the monastery he asked my permission;
I will give him penance for the sin that he committed.

93 It would not be fitting for me to use force against you,
but I appeal to Christ, to His court,
to the One who is almighty and full of wisdom;
I wish to hear this sentence from His lips."

94 The King of Heaven, Wise Judge,
settled this dispute, you never saw it done better:
the Lord ordered the soul returned to the body;
then the sinner would receive whatever reward he deserved.

95 The company was sad and distressed
because of this terrible circumstance that had befallen them;
but the friar, who was already dead, was resuscitated
and everyone was amazed that he was in good condition.

96 The good man spoke to them saying: "Friends,
I was dead and now I am alive, you can be sure of it.
Thanks to the Glorious One who saves Her workers,
She freed me from the hands of the evil warriors!"

97 He told them with his own tongue the whole litany:
what the devils said and what Holy Mary said,
and how She freed him from their power;
if not for Her, he would have been in dark straits.

98 They gave thanks to God with all their hearts,
    and to the Holy Queen, Mother of Mercy,
    who wrought such a miracle out of Her own goodness
    and because of whom Christianity is stronger.

99 The monk confessed and did penance,
    he turned from all his wicked ways,
    he served the Glorious One while he could
    and, when God willed, died without remorse.
    Requiescat in pace cum divina clemencia.[4]

100 Many such miracles and many greater ones
    did Holy Mary work for Her devotees:
    a thousandth of them could not be recounted by any man;
    but for those we can relate, be pleased with us.

---

4. Latin: "May he rest in peace with divine clemency."

❖ Miracle 3
The Cleric and the Flower

101   We read of a cleric who was crackbrained,
    and deeply absorbed in worldly vices;
    but although he was foolish he had one saving grace:
    he loved the Glorious One with all his heart.

102   Even though he had bad habits in other things,
    in greeting Her he was always very prudent;
    he would not go to church nor on any errand
    without first invoking Her name.

103   I could not say what the circumstances were
    for we do not know if he provoked it or not,
    but some enemies attacked this man
    and they killed him. God forgive him!

104   The townspeople as well as his companions
    were not sure how this had come about;
    so, outside the town between some slopes,
    they buried him, and not among Christians.[1]

105   The Virgin was saddened with this burial,
    for Her servant lay excluded from his company.
    She appeared to a cleric of good understanding
    and told him they had erred in this.

106   Full thirty days had he been buried
    (in that length of time his body could be decayed):
    Holy Mary said: "You committed a grave injustice
    in that my scribe lies so far from you.

107   I therefore order you to report that my servant

---

1. *Diezmeros*, tithers, i.e. faithful Christians. Thus, they did not bury him in the cemetery because they were not sure of the circumstances of his death.

did not deserve to be barred from holy ground.
Tell them not to leave him there another thirty days
but to place him with the others in the good cemetery."

108 The cleric, who had been sleeping, asked Her:
"Who are you who speak? Tell me, whom you command,
for when I say this I will be asked
who the aggrieved one is or who the buried one is."

109 The Glorious One responded: "I am Holy Mary,
Mother of Jesus Christ, who suckled My milk.
The one you excluded from your company,
I held as a chancellor of Mine.

110 The one you buried far from the cemetery,
the one to whom you refused Christian burial,
it is on his behalf that I tell all this to you:
if you do not comply, consider yourself in peril."

111 The Lady's command was then carried out:
they opened the grave quickly and with dispatch
and beheld a miracle, not single but double,
the one and the other were immediately well noted.

112 There issued from his mouth a lovely flower—
of very great beauty and very fresh color.
It filled the entire place with a wonderful fragrance;
they did not smell any foul odor from the body.

113 They found his tongue so fresh and sound
that it resembled the inside of a beautiful apple;
it never had been fresher during midday rest
when he would speak in the midst of the orchard.

114 They saw that this had come about because of the Glorious
    One,
for no other could do such a great thing;
they sang *Speciosa*² as they moved his body
near the church to a more precious tomb.

115 Everyone in the world will do a great courtesy
if he does service to the Virgin Mary:
as long as he lives he will see contentment
and he will save his soul on the last day.

---

2. An antiphon in Latin sung in praise of the Virgin Mary (*speciosa* means
"beautiful").

The Virgin's Reward

116　The book tells us of another cleric
　　who loved the image of Holy Mary;
　　he always bowed before Her painting,
　　and felt very great shame under Her gaze.

117　He loved Her Son and he loved Her:
　　he considered the Son as Sun and the Mother as Star;
　　he loved dearly both the Child and the Maiden,
　　but since he served them little, he was very troubled.

118　He learned five phrases, all phrases of joy
　　that speak of the Joys of the Virgin Mary;[1]
　　the cleric recited these before Her each day
　　and She was very well pleased with them.

119　"Joy to you, Mary, who believed the Angel;
　　joy to you, Mary, who as a virgin conceived;
　　joy to you, Mary, who bore the Christ Child;
　　the old law You closed and the new one You opened."

120　As many as there were wounds suffered by the Son,
　　so many Joys did he recite to the One who bore Him;
　　indeed the cleric was good and very deserving,
　　and he received a good reward, a good compensation.

121　In these five Joys we must understand more:
　　five bodily senses that make us sin:

---

1. Here, the five joyful events in the life of the Virgin Mary. Berceo makes specific reference to three: the Annunciation, the Incarnation, and the Nativity. The other two would most likely be the Resurrection and the Assumption.

sight, hearing, smell, taste,
and that of the hands which we call touch.

122   If these five Joys that we have named
we offer freely to the Glorious Mother,
for the error we commit due to these five senses
we will earn pardon through Her holy intercession.

123   This cleric fell gravely ill;
his eyes were about to pop out of his head;
he considered his journey to be complete
and his final hour to be drawing near.

124   The Mother of the Heavenly King appeared to him,
the One who in mercy is without peer;
"Friend," She said to him, "may the Spiritual Father save
     you,
who were His Mother's loyal friend.

125   Take heart, fear not, be not discouraged,
know that you will soon be relieved of this pain;
consider yourself at one with God, free from care,
your pulse now says that it has indeed ended.

126   With Me near you, you need not fear;
consider yourself cured of all the pain;
I always received from you service and love,
and now I wish to repay you for your labor."

127   Indeed the cleric thought he would rise from his bed
and walk through the country on his own feet,
but there is a big difference between thinking and knowing:
this matter was to end in another way.

128   Indeed the cleric thought that he would leave his prison
to make sport and laugh with his friends,
but his soul did not receive such an extension;
it forsook the body, it had to leave it.

129   The Glorious One, Queen of Heaven, took it:
the godchild went with the good Godmother;
and the angels took it with divine grace;
they carried it to Heaven where blessings never cease.

130   What the Glorious Mother promised him,
blessed may She be, She indeed fulfilled;

what She said, he did not understand,
but everything She said turned out true.

131 All who heard the voice and saw this happen
understood that the Glorious One performed a miracle;
they considered the cleric to be very fortunate;
and all glorified the precious Virgin.

The Charitable Pauper

132   There was a poor man who lived off alms.
He had no other income or revenue
except on rare occasions when he worked;
he had in his bag very few pennies.

133   To win the favor of the Glorious One, Whom he loved
        dearly,
he shared with the poor everything he earned;
in this he strove and in this struggled;
to win Her favor he forgot his own needs.

134   When this pauper had to pass from this world
the Glorious Mother came to greet him,
She spoke to him very sweetly, She wanted to praise him,
everyone in the town heard Her words:

135   "You have coveted our company a great deal
and have earned it with very good skill
for you have shared your alms, you have said 'Ave Maria';
I indeed understood why you did it all.

136   Be assured that your job is well done,
this day we are in is your last;
consider sung the *Ite missa est* sung,[1]
the time has come to collect your wages.

137   I have come here to take you with me
to the kingdom of my Son who is indeed your friend,

---

1. The final words of the mass, "Go, mass is over," here used metaphorically to indicate the end of the poor man's life.

there where the angels feed on good wheat bread;
the Holy Virtues[2] will be pleased with you."

138   When the Glorious One had finished the sermon,
the soul abandoned the fortunate body.
An honored band of angels took it
and carried it to Heaven—God therefore be praised!

139   The men who had heard the voice before,
at once saw the promise fulfilled;
each in his own way gave thanks
to the Glorious Mother who is so prudent.

140   Unfortunate would be the one who heard such a thing
without being extremely pleased with Holy Mary.
If he did not honor Her more, he would be impudent.
The one who parts from Her is sorely deceived.

141   We wish to move on even further;
a lesson such as this must not be cut short,
for these are the trees in which we must take pleasure,
in whose shade the birds are accustomed to sing.[3]

---

2. The second choir of the second hierarchy of angels.

3. Here Berceo pauses to refer back to the trees, shade, and birds of the allegorical Introduction.

❖ Miracle 6

The Devout Thief

142   There was a bad thief who would rather steal
than go to church or build bridges;[1]
he knew how to maintain his house by theft,
a bad habit that he took up and could not quit.

143   If he committed other sins we do not read about them;
it would be wrong to condemn him for what we do not know;
let what we have said to you suffice:
if he did more, may Christ in Whom we believe pardon him!

144   Among his other evils, he did have one good habit,
which availed him in the end and gave him salvation:
he believed in the Glorious One with all his heart;
he always greeted Her facing Her Majesty.

145   He said "Hail, Mary" and more of the prayer,[2]
he always bowed before Her image,
and felt very great shame under Her gaze;
in so doing he felt his soul was more secure.[3]

146   As he who walks in evil in evil must fall,
this thief was caught with stolen goods;
and as he had no way to defend himself,
he was sentenced to be hanged on the gallows.

---

1. Building and maintaining bridges was one of the civic duties of medieval man. See Alfonso el Sabio, *Siete Partidas* (1807; Madrid: Atlas, 1972) 1.6.54, and 3.32.20.

2. The "Ave Maria" was not a single fixed prayer during Berceo's time; rather there were versions of different lengths. This remark indicates that the thief's devotion led him to pray a longer version.

3. There are different versions of this strophe. We have followed Dutton's edition.

147 The constable took him to the crossroads
where the gallows had been erected by council;
they covered his eyes with a well-tied cloth,
and raised him from the ground with a tightly drawn rope.

148 They raised him from the ground as high as they could,
those who were nearby considered him dead;
if they had known before what they later learned,
they would not have done what they did to him.

149 The Glorious Mother, skilled in aid,
who is accustomed to helping Her servants in trouble,
wished to protect this condemned man;
She remembered the service that he always rendered Her.

150 As he was hanging, under his feet She placed
Her precious hands and gave him relief;
he did not feel burdened by anything at all
and had never been more comfortable or more content.

151 Then on the third day his relatives came,
and with them his friends and acquaintances;
they came, with faces scratched[4] and grieving, to take him
    down;
but the situation was better than they thought.

152 They found him alive, happy, and unharmed.
He would not have been so comfortable had he been lying
    in a bath;
he said that under his feet there was a certain footstool
and that he would not feel any pain if he hung there a year.

153 When the ones who had hanged him heard this,
they thought that the noose had been faulty;
they regretted that they had not cut his throat:
that would have pleased them as much as what they later
    enjoyed.

154 That entire band was of the same mind:
they had been foiled by the bad noose,
but they should now cut his throat with sickle or sword
so that their town would not be shamed by a thief!

---

4. The scratching of the face in the Middle Ages was an outward indication
of grief over loss through death. See Dutton *Obras* 2:73, note 151c.

155 The most agile young men went to cut his throat
with strong blades, long and sharp;
but Holy Mary interposed Her hands
and the gullet of his throat remained intact.

156 When they saw that they could do him no harm,
that the Glorious Mother wished to protect him,
they withdrew from the dispute
and until God willed otherwise they let him live.

157 They allowed him to go his way in peace,
for they did not wish to oppose Holy Mary;
he bettered his ways and set folly aside,
completed his life and died when his time came.[5]

158 Mother so compassionate, of such benevolence,
Who has mercy on the good and the bad,
we should bless Her with all our heart
for those who did bless Her earned great riches.

159 The skills of the Mother and those of Him Whom She bore
are exactly alike to the one who knows them well;
He descended for all—the good and the bad;
She came to the aid of all who called upon Her.

---

5. He died a natural death.

❖ MIRACLE 7

Saint Peter and the Proud Monk

160   In rich Cologne, a royal capital,[1]
there was a monastery called Saint Peter's;
therein lived an undisciplined monk
who cared little for what the rule[2] says.

161   He had very little sense, he committed much foolishness;
although they punished him, he was incorrigible;
because of this a great misfortune befell him:
a harlot bore a child by him.

162   For his body's sake and to live more soundly,
he used electuaries[3] every day:
in winter warm ones and in summer cold;
he should have been devout, but he was lusty.

163   In this life he lived in great agitation
and died of his sins, for his grave excesses;
he neither took *Corpus Domini*[4] nor made confession,
so the devils carried his soul off to prison.

164   Saint Peter the Apostle took pity on him,
for the monk had been ordained in his monastery;

---

1. Cologne was the capital of the electoral principality of the Rhine.

2. Reference to the monastic rule (i.e., laws or regulations) by which the religious order was governed.

3. Electuaries were medicines prepared in a base of honey. Their use in the Middle Ages to control the libido of the clergy gives Berceo's reference a double meaning.

4. Latin for "body of Christ," a reference to the Holy Eucharist.

and he prayed to Jesus Christ with great devotion
that He might extend to him a portion of His mercy.

165 Jesus Christ said: "Peter, my beloved,
you know very well what David said in his book:
that he shall dwell in the Holy Hill[5]
who enters without stain and free from sin.

166 That one for whom you pray on bended knee
neither behaved righteously nor lived without stain;
the monastery gained nothing from his company;
he must sit in the chair he has earned!"[6]

167 Saint Peter prayed to the Heavenly Virtues,[7]
that they might implore the Father of Penitents
to remove this man from his mortal bonds;
He responded in the same words as before.

168 He turned to the Glorious Mother of Our Lord,
and to the other virgins of Her house;
they went to Christ in great supplication;
they prayed for the soul of the monk.

169 When Lord Christ saw his Glorious Mother
and such a beautiful procession of Her friends,
He came out to receive them in a lovely way;
the soul who beheld this would be blessed indeed.

170 "Mother," said Lord Christ, "I would like to know
what matter brings you here with this company."
"Son," said the Mother, "I have come to beg you
for the soul of a monk from a certain monastery."

171 "Mother," said the Son, "it would not be right
for the soul of such a man to enter into such delight;
the entire Scripture would be discredited,
but since it is Your request, we will find a solution.

172 I will do so for love of You:
let it return to the body where it dwelt;
let him make penance as sinners do;
thus, in a better way, can he be saved."

---

5. Psalms 15:1: "Lord, who shall abide in thy tabernacle? who shall dwell in thy holy hill?"

6. He must be punished or rewarded according to his merits.

7. The heavenly virtues are one of the orders of angels.

173   When Saint Peter heard this sweet command,
and saw his petition had ended happily,
he turned to the devils, that malevolent band:
he wrested from them the soul they were carrying.

174   He gave it to two children of great brightness,
angelic creatures of great holiness;
into their charge he willingly gave it
to be returned to the body in all safety.

175   The children gave it to an honored friar
who from childhood had been reared in the order;[8]
the friar took it to the body which was laid out enshrouded;
and the monk revived. May God be praised!

176   The guide, that is, the good friar I just mentioned,
said to the soul of the monk,
"I beg you for God's sake and Holy Mary's
to pray for me every day.

177   Another thing do I request: that my grave,
now all covered with trash,
please be so kind as to have it swept clean:
do this and may God give you good fortune!"

178   The monk, the one who was dead, revived
but for one whole day remained quite addled;
however, he finally regained all of his wits
and relayed to the community what had happened.

179   They offered thanks to God, to the regal Virgin,
and to the holy apostle, keeper of Heaven's keys,
who endured censure to save his monk;
this was no miracle of ordinary value!

180   May no one harbor doubt within his heart
nor say that this thing could or could not be.
Let him fix his understanding on the Glorious One
and he will comprehend that this does not defy reason.

181   Since the Glorious One is full of mercy,
full of grace and free from vassalage,[9]
no request would ever be denied Her;
such a Son would never tell such a Mother "No."

---

8. The friar-guide is dead; it is his spirit that ultimately delivers the monk's soul to his body.

9. The Virgin Mary is her own mistress; she is vassal of no one.

❖ MIRACLE 8

The Pilgrim Deceived by the Devil

182   Gentlefolk and friends, for God's and charity's sake,
      hear another miracle, which is truly lovely;
      Saint Hugh, abbot of Cluny,[1] wrote it
      for it happened to a monk of his order.

183   A friar of his house who was called Guiralt
      before becoming a monk was not very wise;
      sometimes he committed the folly and sin
      of an unmarried man without obligations.

184   He decided one day, there where he was,
      to go on a pilgrimage to the Apostle of Spain;[2]
      he arranged his affairs, and looked for his companions;
      they determined when and how they would make their way.

185   When they were about to leave he did a vile thing:
      instead of keeping vigil, he lay with his mistress.
      He did not do penance as the law says
      and set out on the way with this stinging nettle.[3]

---

1. Saint Hugh (1024-1109) became abbot of Cluny in 1049 at the age of twenty-five. Adviser to contemporary sovereigns and popes, he ruled over more than a thousand monasteries and dependencies.

2. Saint James the Greater, whose shrine at Compostela was one of the leading pilgrimage destinations during the Middle Ages. See our Introduction.

3. Literally, an "evil nettle" (*mala hortiga*), used here figuratively to refer to his sin. The nettle is a plant armed with stinging or prickly hairs. Thus, the pilgrim sets out with the irritating "nettle" or "sin" since he did not repent and free himself of it.

186   He had covered only a little of the journey,
it was perhaps about the third day,
when he had an encounter along the way
that appeared to be good, though in truth it was not.

187   The old Devil was always a traitor
and is a skillful master of all sin;
sometimes he appears as an angel of the Creator
but he is a cunning devil, an enticer to evil.

188   The false one transformed himself into the semblance of
an angel,
and stood before the pilgrim in the midst of a path:
"Welcome, my friend," he said to the pilgrim,
"you seem to me a little thing, innocent like a lamb.

189   You left your house to come to mine,
but upon leaving you committed a folly.
You intend to complete the pilgrimage without penance—
Holy Mary will not reward you for this!"

190   "Who are you, sir?" the pilgrim said to him.
And he responded: "I am James, son of Zebedee.
Be aware, friend, that you are wandering astray;
it seems you have no desire to save yourself."

191   Guiralt said: "Well, sir, what do you command?
I want to comply with all that you tell me,
for I see that I have committed great iniquities,
I did not do the penance that the abbots dictate."

192   The false James responded: "This is my judgment:
that you cut off the parts of your body that commit
fornication;
then cut your throat: thus will you do service to God,
for you will make sacrifice to him of your very flesh."

193   The ill-starred one, crazed and foolish, believed him;
he took out his knife that he had sharpened;
the poor crazy wretch cut off his genitals;
then he slit his own throat and died excommunicated.

194   When the companions with whom he had set out
arrived to where Guiralt was and saw him like that,
they were in greater affliction than they ever had been;
how this had come to pass they could not imagine!

195 They saw that his throat had not been cut by thieves
since they had taken nothing from him nor robbed him;
he had not been challenged by anyone;
they did not know how this had come about.

196 They all quickly fled and scattered;
they thought they would be suspected of this death;
even though they were not guilty of the deed,
perhaps they would be taken prisoner and accused.

197 The one who gave the advice, together with his followers,
big and little, small and large,
falsehearted traitors, they shackled his soul
and were carrying it to the fire, to the cruel sweats.

198 They were carrying it, and not gently;
Saint James, whose pilgrimage it was, saw it;
he came out in great haste to the road
and stood before them in the front rank.

199 "Free," he said, "oh, evil ones, the prisoner that you carry,
for he is not quite as surely yours as you think;
hold him carefully; do not use force against him.
I believe you cannot even if you try."

200 A devil retorted, he stood there obstinately:
"James, you are trying to make mock of all of us;
you want to go against what is right,
you have some wicked scheme under your scapular.

201 Guiralt committed a sin, he killed himself with his own hand,
he must be judged as a brother of Judas;[4]
he is in all ways our parishioner;
James, do not try to be villainous towards us!"

202 Saint James said to him: "Treacherous tongue wagger,
your speech cannot be worth a bogus coin;
using my voice, as a false advocate
you gave bad advice, you killed my pilgrim!

203 Had you not told him that you were Saint James,
had you not shown him the sign of my scallop shells,[5]

---

4. Judas Iscariot who betrayed Christ committed suicide (Matthew 27.5).

5. An attribute of Saint James of Compostela, the scallop shell was also worn as a badge by his pilgrims.

he would not have harmed his body with his own scissors
nor would he lie as he lies, outside in the road.

204 I am greatly offended by your behavior;
I consider my image mocked by you;
you killed my pilgrim with a skillful lie.
Moreover, I see his soul mistreated.

205 Let me await the judgment of the Virgin Mary:
I appeal to Her in this case;
otherwise I will never be rid of you,
for I see that you bring very great treachery."

206 They presented their arguments before the Glorious One,
the matter was well stated by each party.
The Precious Queen understood the arguments
and the dispute ended appropriately:

207 "The deceit that he suffered must be held in his favor,
he thought he was obeying Saint James,
and that in so doing he would be saved;
the deceiver should suffer more."

208 She said: "I order this and give it as judgment:
the soul over which you have the dispute
shall return to its body and do penance,
then as he merits shall he be judged."

209 This sentence was carried out, it was sanctioned by God.
The wretched soul was returned to the body;
even though it grieved the Devil and all his band,
the soul went back to its former abode.

210 The body, which was lying there dazed, arose.
Guiralt of the slit throat cleaned his face
and stood there a short while like someone bewildered,
like a man who is sleeping and awakens annoyed.

211 As for the wound he had from the throat-cutting,
its scar barely showed,
and all pain and fever had ended.
Everyone said: "This man was indeed fortunate!"

212 Of everything else he was healed and mended,
except for a tiny line that crossed him,
but his private parts, all that were cut off,
never grew back one bit and he remained in that condition.

213 He was completely sound, with everything healed over,
and, for passing water, the hole remained.
He requested those provisions that he had been carrying on
his back.
He prepared to go on his way, happy and content.

214 He gave thanks to God and to Holy Mary
and to the holy apostle whose pilgrimage he was making;
he made haste and found his company:
they had this miracle for comfort each day.

215 This great marvel was sounded throughout Compostela,
and all the townspeople came out to see him
saying: "Such a thing as this we must write down,
those who are yet to come will take pleasure in hearing it."

216 When he went back to his homeland, having finished the
journey,
and people heard what had happened,
there was great commotion, they were moved
upon seeing this Lazarus returned from death to life.[6]

217 And this pilgrim pondered his fortune:
how God had delivered him from the wicked teeth.
He abandoned the world, friends and relatives;
he entered the abbey of Cluny; he dressed in a penitent's
habit.

218 Hugh, a good man, abbot of Cluny,
a religious man of very great holiness,
told this miracle that truly happened.
He put it in writing; he did an honorable thing.

219 Guiralt died in the order, leading a good life,
serving the Creator in word and in deed,
persevering in good, repenting of sin.
The evil enemy did not go off laughing at him.[7]
For all that he had sinned, he made good amends to God.

---

6. Lazarus, the brother of Mary and Martha, was resuscitated by Christ
after being dead for days (John 11.1-44).

7. The evil enemy is the devil.

❖ MIRACLE 9

The Simple Cleric

220   There was a simple cleric of little learning;
      daily he said Holy Mary's mass;
      he did not know how to say any other, he said it each day;
      he knew it more by habit than through understanding.

221   This officiant was denounced to the bishop
      as an idiot, a plainly bad cleric.
      He only said the "Salve Sancta Parens";[1]
      the impaired dullard knew no other mass.

222   The bishop was harshly moved to rage
      and said: "Never did I hear such a deed of a priest."
      He said, "Tell the son of the evil whore
      to appear before me—do not postpone it through some ploy!"

223   The sinful priest came before the bishop;
      with his great fear, he had lost his color;
      from shame he could not look at his seigneur—
      never was the wretch in such a bad sweat.

224   The bishop said to him: "Priest, tell me the truth,
      is your stupidity such as they say?"
      The good man responded: "Sir, for charity's sake,
      if I said 'No,' I would be telling a lie."

225   The bishop said: "Since you do not have the knowledge
      to sing another Mass—nor the wit or the ability—
      I forbid you to sing, and I give you this sentence:
      live as befits you, by some other means."

---

1. *Salve Sancta Parens*, Latin: "Greetings, Holy Parent," the initial words
of the introit for the Nativity of the Virgin, celebrated on September 8.

226 The priest went his way, sad and disheartened;
he felt very great shame and very great hurt;
weeping and moaning he turned to the Glorious One
so that She might advise him, for he was dismayed.

227 The merciful Mother, who never failed
anyone who fell at Her feet in sincerity,
immediately heard the plea of Her cleric;
She did not put it off and helped him at once.

228 The merciful Virgin, Mother free from sin,
appeared to the bishop immediately in a vision;
She spoke strong words to him, a very angry sermon;
She revealed the desire of Her heart in it.

229 She said to him irately: "Imperious Bishop,
why were you so harsh and villainous to me?
I never took a grain's-worth from you,
and you have taken a chaplain from me!

230 The one who sang Mass to me each day
you held that he was committing an act of heresy;
you judged him a beast and a thing astray;
you took from him the order of chaplaincy.[2]

231 If you do not order him to say my Mass
as he was accustomed to say it, there will be a great quarrel
and you will be dead on the thirtieth day.
Then you will see what the wrath of Holy Mary is worth!"

232 With these threats the bishop was terrified,
immediately he sent for the banned priest;
he begged his pardon for the error he had made,
for he was, in his case, badly deceived.

233 The bishop ordered him to sing as he had been accustomed
to sing,
and to be the servant of the Glorious One at Her altar;
should he lack anything in the way of clothing or shoes,
he would order it given him from his very own.

234 The good man returned to his chaplaincy,
he served the Glorious One, Holy Mother Mary;

---

2. To remove the order of chaplaincy is to prohibit from celebrating mass.

he died in office, a death that I would like:
his soul went to Heaven, to the sweet society.

235   We could not write or pray enough,
even if we could endure for many years,
to be able to relate a tenth of the miracles
that, through the Glorious One, God deigns to show.

The Two Brothers

236 In the town of Rome, that noble city,
mistress and lady of all Christendom,
there were two brothers of great authority:
one was a cleric, the other a magistrate.

237 They called the cleric Pedro—that was his name—
a wise and noble man, one of the Pope's cardinals:
among his vices, he had one that was unpardonable;
he was very greedy, a mortal sin.

238 The second brother had the name of Estevan;
among senators none was more proud;
he was a very powerful Roman,
and in *prendo prendis*[1] he had a well-practiced hand.

239 He was very covetous—he wanted very much to possess;
he falsified judgments out of desire for property;
he took from people what he could take;
he valued money more than maintaining justice.

240 With the pronouncement of false judgments,
he took three properties from Saint Lawrence the Martyr;[2]
Saint Agnes[3] lost on his account goodly places,
an orchard that was worth many pairs of coins.

---

1. *Prendo prendis*: first two elements of the Latin paradigm for *prendere* (to take): I take, you take. . . . Use of the phrase indicates that Estevan stole from others.

2. An early Christian saint, born near Huesca in Spain. Martyred in Rome in 258 and, according to legend, roasted alive on a gridiron in the presence of the emperor. He is the subject of Berceo's *Martyrdom of Saint Lawrence*.

3. Fourth-century virgin martyr who died around 350 at the age of twelve.

241   The cardinal, Pedro the Honest, died
       and went to purgatory where he deserved to be taken;
       within a few days Estevan died,
       he expected the type of judgment that he had given.

242   Saint Lawrence saw him and looked at him in an ugly way;
       he squeezed his arm hard three times;
       Estevan complained from way down in his belly.
       Iron pincers would not have squeezed so tightly.

243   Saint Agnes saw the one who had taken her orchard,[4]
       she turned her back on him, she looked at him with a wry
              face;
       then Estevan said: "This is little comfort,
       all our profit has brought us to a bad port."[5]

244   God, our Lord, Just Judge,
       the One from Whom neither wine cellar nor pantry is hidden,
       said that this man was a wicked crossbowman;
       he blinded many men, not just one.

245   "He dispossessed many through false advocacy;
       because of his sins he always schemed treachery.
       He does not deserve to enter Our company,
       let him go lie with Judas in that infirmary!"[6]

246   The ancient warriors[7] took him in bonds,
       those who always were our mortal enemies;
       they gave him for his portion, not apples or figs,
       but smoke and vinegar, wounds and pinches.

247   He saw his brother with other sinners,
       where the wretch was in very bad sweats;
       he let out cries and shouts, tears and lamentations.
       He had a great abundance of evil servants.

248   They had already carried the soul near to the dwelling
(249)   place,
           where it never would see a thing that would please it,

---

4. Estevan is the one who took the orchard.

5. Our profit has brought us to a bad end, to ruin.

6. Hell.

7. The devils.

nor would it see sun or moon or goodly dew,
and he would be in darkness like an anchorite.

249 He said to him: "Say, brother, I wish to ask you:
(248) for what fault do you lie in such terrible misery,
for if God is willing and I can do it
I will seek help for you in all the ways that I know."

250 Pedro said: "In life I had great avarice.
I had it, as though it were a mistress, along with covetousness;
for that reason I am now placed in such sadness.
'As one works, so let one be paid,' that is law and justice.[8]

251 But, if the Pope and his clergy
sang mass for me for just one day,
I, trusting in the Glorious One, Holy Mother Mary,
know that God, straightway, would improve my lot."

252 Although this man Estevan, about whom we speak so much,
carried many injustices under his cloak,
he had one good quality: he loved a saint
so much that we could not show you how much.

253 He loved Projectus,[9] martyr of great worth,
he kept his feast day well, as befitting a good lord;
he gave him a splendid Mass and did him very great honor
and for the poor and for clerics did as much good as he
could.[10]

254 Lawrence and Agnes, although offended
because he had earlier dispossessed them,
were moved to pity and were mollified,
they looked more to God than at his sins.

255 They went to Projectus, whose devotee he had been,
they said to him: "Projectus, do not be caught napping.
Think about your Estevan who is being scorned;
give him a reward for having served you!"

256 He went to the Glorious One Who shines more than a star,

---

8. One gets one's just deserts. This is a motif seen in many of the miracle tales.

9. Probably Saint Projectus, Bishop of Imola (fifth century).

10. The Latin source indicates that Estevan (Stephanus) gave alms to the poor and fed the clergy. For the Latin see Dutton *Obras* 2:101.

he moved Her with great pleading and went before God
    with Her.
He prayed for this soul that they were carrying like a ball,
    that it might not be judged according to the complaint.

257   God, Our Lord, replied to this supplication:
    "I will grant such a favor because of your love;
    let the sinful soul return to the body,
    henceforth, it will receive whatever honor it deserves.

258   Let there be a time limit of thirty days,
    so that he may correct all his errors,
    and indeed I affirm to him by My words,
    that all his misdeeds will end."

259   The petitioners rendered *Gratias multas*[11] to God
    because he had mercy on His sinners
    and freed this soul from wicked traitors
    who are ever deceivers of the faithful.

260   When the diabolical band heard that,
    they let go the soul that they had bound;
    Saint Projectus who had won it back took it
    and led it to its body, to its dwelling place.

261   The Glorious One, Mother of the Creator, said:
    "Estevan, give thanks to God the Good Lord,
    He has granted you a great favor, which could not be
        greater;
    if you do not watch yourself, you will fall from bad into
        worse.

262   Estevan, I still want to give you some advice
    and, Estevan, it is advice that you must take:
    I order you to recite a psalm each day:
    'Beati inmaculati . . .'[12] which is very good to pray.

263   If you say this Psalm each morning
    and right the wrongs that you did to the churches,
    your soul will win glory when you die;
    you will avoid the punishment and the somber places."

---

11. Latin: "Many thanks."

12. "Blessed are the undefiled . . .," first words of Psalm 118 (119 in King
James version).

264 Estevan revived—thanks be to Jesus Christ!
He related to the Pope all that he had seen,
what Pedro, his beloved brother, had said to him,
and how he had lain in great torment, miserable and very sad.

265 He showed his arm that was bruised,
the one that Saint Lawrence had squeezed.
With body prostrated, he asked a favor of the Pope:
that he say Mass for the suffering Pedro.

266 So that they might believe and he might be believed,
he said that after thirty days he would be dead;
everyone said: "This is a certain sign;
it will indeed be known if you are telling the truth or not."

267 He made rich restitution to the disinherited ones,
he satisfied well those whom he had wronged;
he confessed all his sins to the priest—
all those he had done and spoken and thought.

268 When the four weeks were coming to an end
and there were only a few mornings before the thirty days
elapsed,
Estevan bade farewell to the Roman people;
he knew God's words would not prove to be vain.

269 On the thirtieth day he made his confession,
he received *Corpus Domini* with great devotion;
he lay down on his bed, said his prayer,
surrendered his soul to God and died blessed.

❖ MIRACLE 11

The Greedy Farmer

270   There was in a certain region a farmer man
who did more plowing than any other labor;
he loved the land more than he did the Creator,
in many ways he was a rebellious man.

271   He committed a sin, a truly dirty one:
he changed the boundary markers to gain land,
in all ways did he commit injustice and deceit;
he had a bad reputation in his region.

272   Although wicked, he loved Holy Mary;
he heard Her miracles and welcomed them;
he always greeted Her; each day he said:
"Hail to thee, full of grace, Who bore the Messiah!"

273   The hayseed died owning much land,
he was immediately captured by the devils' rope;
they dragged him bound and thoroughly mauled,
making him pay double for the bread that he had stolen.

274   As the devils carried this wretched soul away,
the angels took pity on it;
they wanted to help it, to make it one of their own,
but they did not have the flour for making such a dough.

275   If the angels gave them one good argument,
the others gave a hundred bad arguments instead of good ones;
the wicked ones had the good in a corner;
the soul because of its sins did not come out of prison.

276   One angel got up and said: "I am a witness,
and this that I tell you is the truth, not a lie:

the body that had this soul with it
was a vassal and friend of Holy Mary!

277   He always mentioned Her at dinner and supper,
he would say three words: *Ave gratia plena*[1]:
the mouth from which came such a hallowed song
did not deserve to lie in so wicked a chain."

278   As soon as this name of the Holy Queen
was heard by the demons, they promptly withdrew from
      there;
they all dispersed like a mist,
all abandoned the wretched soul.

279   The angels saw it being abandoned,
its feet and hands well bound with ropes;
it was like a sheep that lies trapped in brambles;
they went and led it back to the fold.

280   O name so blessed and so virtuous
that can chase and frighten away the enemy!
Our hurting tongues and throats should not
keep any of us from saying "Salve Regina Sancta."[2]

---

1. Latin: "Hail, full of grace."

2. Reference to the hymn "Salve Regina, mater misericordiae."

❖ MIRACLE 12

The Prior and
Uberto the Sexton

281 In a good town that they call Pavia,[1]
a town of great wealth that lies in Lombardy,
there was a rich monastery
of many good men, a very holy company.

282 The monastery was erected in honor
of the One who saved the world, the Holy Savior;[2]
there happened to be a prior in it
who only wanted to live exactly as he pleased.

283 The good man had an erring tongue,
he said much filth, which is forbidden by the rule;[3]
he did not lead a very ordered life
but did say his hours[4] in serenity.

284 He had one custom that profited him:
he said all his hours like a proper monk;
for those of the Glorious One he always stood;
and for that reason the devil felt great animosity toward him.

285 Although in some things he seemed dull
and, as we told you, he was foulmouthed,

---

1. City in Lombardy, a region in the north of Italy, today capital of the province of Pavia.

2. Reference to the monastery of San Salvador of Pavia, founded in the tenth century.

3. Reference to the monastic rule.

4. Canonical hours, times of day set for prayer.

in loving the Glorious One he was quite devout;
he said Her office *de suo corde toto.*[5]

286 When God willed it, this prior died;
he fell into exile, in a harsh place;
no one could tell you the misery
that the prior bore, nor could one imagine it!

287 There was a sexton in that abbey
who looked after the things of the sacristy;
he was called Uberto, a prudent man and without folly,
because of him the monastery was worth more, not less!

288 Before matins, very early one morning,
this monk arose to say the matin prayer,
to ring matins, to awaken the company,
to set up the lamps, to light the dwelling.

289 The prior of the house, mentioned above,
had been dead for a year,
but his case was finally reviewed
as carefully as on the day he was buried.

290 The monk of the house who was the sexton,
before he began ringing the monitory bell[6]
was cleaning the lamps to provide better light,
when he took great fright in a strange manner.

291 He heard a man's weak, tired voice;
it said "Friar Ubert" more than once;
Ubert recognized it and did not doubt at all
that it was the prior's; he took great fright.

292 He went out of the church; he went to the infirmary,
his spirit was not free of fear,
were he going on a pilgrimage he would not have moved
      faster,
Sir Fear was driving him, by my head![7]

293 Being in such a state, out of his wits,
he heard, "Ubert, Ubert, why do you not answer me?

---

5. Latin: "with all his heart."

6. The "warning bell" that sounds the call for the canonical hours.

7. A mild oath.

Look, have no fear; by no means be afraid;
consider how to speak to me and how to question me."

294 Then Ubert said: "Prior, by your faith,
tell me about yourself, how you are,
so that the chapter will know
what state you are in or what state you expect."

295 The prior said: "Ubert, my servant,
know that up to now my state has been miserable;
I fell into a place of exile, cruel and unpleasant.
The prince of the land was called Smirna.[8]

296 I suffered great misery; I spent a very bad time.
I could not tell you the evil I have suffered;
but Holy Mary passed by there,
She felt grief and sorrow for the harm I was suffering.

297 She took me by the hand and carried me with her;
She led me to a serene and sheltering place.
She freed me from oppression of the mortal enemy;
She put me in a place where I will live without peril.

298 Thanks be to the Glorious One who is full of grace!
I am free from misery, I have come out of suffering;
I fell into a sweet garden near a sweet beehive,[9]
where I will see no lack of dinner or supper."

299 With that, the voice became silent and the monastery
    awoke;
they all went to the church with good will.
They said matins and prayers of intercession
in a manner that would please God.

300 Matins sung, the day dawned;
then they said prime[10] and afterward the litany;
the holy company went to the chapter house
obeying the rule, the custom of monks.

---

8. A name for the devil, the prince of darkness, but the precise origin of its
use here is unknown. The name Smirna appears in the Latin source and
there is reference to Smyrna in Revelation 2.8, where those who claim to be
Jews but are not truly righteous are the "synagogue of Satan."

9. The garden motif evokes the "garden paradise" of Berceo's Introduction.

10. The second of the canonical hours, after matins.

301   Being in the chapter meeting and the lesson read,
      the sexton made his genuflection;
      he related to the assembly the entire vision,
      weeping with very good reason.

302   All gave thanks to the Glorious Mother
      Who to Her vassals is always merciful;
      they went to the church singing a beautiful hymn.
      They had the whole story set down in writing.

303   After a little while, the sexton died;
      he died a death that God grants every Christian;
      he left harsh winter; he entered fair summer;
      he went to paradise where he will be forever safe.

304   This is *summum bonum*[11] to serve such a Lady,
      Who knows how to aid Her servants in such an hour;
      this Lady is a good shelter; She is a good shepherdess;
      She helps everyone who prays to Her with a good heart.

305   All who heard of this vision
      gathered into their souls greater devotion,
      loving the Glorious One with a better heart
      and calling upon Her in their tribulations.

---

11. Latin: "the supreme or highest good."

Jerónimo, the New Bishop of Pavia

306   In that same city,[1] there was a good Christian,
      he was named Jerónimo, he was a Mass-singer;[2]
      he did daily service to the Glorious One,
      day and night, winter and summer.

307   By chance the bishop of the place died;
      another one could not be agreed upon at all;
      they held a triduum,[3] they wanted to pray to God
      so that He might show them whom they should elevate.

308   To a very religious and Catholic man,
      the Glorious One spoke and said in a vision:
      "Young man, why are you in such dissension?
      Give this election to my devotee."

309   The good man said to Her, to be very sure:
      "Who are you who speak or who is the devotee?"
      "I am," She said, "the Mother of the True God;
      they call my key-keeper[4] Jerónimo.

310   Be my messenger, take this order:

---

1. Pavia, the town in which the previous miracle (no. 12) takes place.

2. That is, a priest who officiates at mass.

3. A religious exercise in which three days are spent in prayer, fasting, and other acts of devotion.

4. Since one of the duties of the key-keeper, or keeper of the keys, is to defend the monastery with its sacred objects, the term may indicate that the Virgin sees Jerónimo in this light.

      I command you to carry it out quickly;
      if the council does otherwise they will be badly mistaken,
      My Son will not be pleased with their action."

311 She said this and the electors believed it,
      but who Jerónimo was they did not know.
      They posted spies throughout the town;
      they were going to give a good reward to the identifiers.

312 They found Jerónimo, a parish priest,
      a man without great deeds but who knew little of evil;
      they led him by the hand to the cathedral seat,
      they gave him as his portion the bishop's throne.

313 Following the message that Holy Mary gave,
      they made him bishop and lord of Pavia;
      in that, everyone took great pleasure and joy,
      for they saw that it had come about in a good way.

314 He was a very good bishop and a just shepherd,
      a lion to the fierce and, to the meek, a lamb;
      he guided his flock well, not like a hireling,
      but as a firm shepherd who takes the lead.

315 God our Lord guided his works;
      he had a good life, and a much better death;
      when he departed this world he went to the greater one,
      the Glorious One led him, Mother of the Creator.

316 Mother so merciful, may She always be praised,
      may She always be blessed and ever adored,
      for She places Her friends in such high regard.
      Her mercy can never be appreciated!

The Image Miraculously Spared by the Flames

317   San Miguel de la Tumba[1] is a great monastery;
       it lies surrounded, completely encircled by the sea,
       in a perilous place where great hardships are suffered
       by the monks who live there.

318   In this monastery that we have named,
       there were good monks, a well-proven community,
       and a sumptuous and very honored altar of the Glorious One
       that held a precious image of very great value.

319   The image was posed on Her throne,
       Her Son in Her arms, in the customary fashion;
       with the kings[2] around Her, She was well accompanied,
       like a rich queen, sanctified by God.

320   Like a wealthy queen, She wore a valuable crown;
       over it was an elegant wimple instead of a veil;
       it was beautifully cut and of very fine work,
       and it brought honor to the town nearby.

321   There was hanging in front of it a lovely fan,
       in the common tongue they call it a *moscadero;*[3]

---

1. San Miguel de la Tumba refers to Mont-Saint-Michel, an island monastery in France located between Normandy and Brittany. The name was changed to Mont-Saint-Michel in the eighth century.

2. Images of the Magi, the three kings who came from the East to worship the Christ-child (Matthew 2.1 ff.)

3. A fan for shooing flies (Spanish *moscas*).

its craftsman had made it of peacock's feathers,
it shone like stars, like the Morning Star.

322 A lightning bolt came out of the sky because of the grave sins,
it burned the church on all four sides,
it burned all the books and sacred cloths,
and the monks themselves were almost burned.

323 It burned the cupboards and the frontals,[4]
the beams, the cross braces, the rafters, the ridgepieces,
the altar cruets,[5] chalices, and processional candlesticks;
God suffered that calamity as He does others.

324 Although the fire was so strong and so scorching,
it did not reach the Lady nor did it reach the Child,
nor did it reach the fan that was hanging in front;
it did them not a penny's worth of damage.

325 The image did not burn nor did the flabellum[6] burn,
nor did they suffer a hair's worth of harm.
Not even the smoke reached it;
it did not harm it any more than I would harm Bishop Tello.[7]

326 *Continens et contentum*[8] were completely ruined,
everything was turned to ash, it was all destroyed;
but around the image for as much as an *estado*[9]
the fire had dared do no damage.

327 Everyone took this as an extraordinary marvel,
that neither smoke nor fire reached Her,
that the flabellum remained brighter than a star,
the Child still beautiful and still beautiful the Maiden.

328 The precious miracle did not fall into oblivion,
it was immediately well dictated and put into writing;

---

4. Hanging for the front of an altar.

5. Cruets for the wine and the water at mass.

6. The fan.

7. Tello Téllez de Meneses, bishop of Palencia, died in 1246. Berceo is thought to have studied in Palencia.

8. Latin: "the container and its contents."

9. *Estado*, Spanish: a linear measurement of approximately seven feet or a surface measurement of forty-nine square feet.

as long as the world exists, it will be told;
because of this, a calamity was converted into a blessing.

329   The Blessed Virgin, General Queen,
just as She freed Her wimple from this fire,
so does She free Her servants from the everlasting fire;
She takes them to Heaven where they shall never know evil.

The Wedding and the Virgin

330   In the town of Pisa, an illustrious city
that lies on a seaport[1] and is extremely wealthy,
there was a canon of good lineage;
the place where he lived was called Saint Cassian's.

331   As did others about whom we have told above,
who were chaplains of Holy Mary,
this one loved Her very much, more than many Christians,
and served Her with his hands and his feet.

332   At that time the clergy did not have the custom
of saying any hours to You, Virgin Mary,
but he said them always and each day;
in the Glorious One he took pleasure and delight.

333   His parents had only this one son,
so when they died he was their heir.
They left him very valuable holdings in personal property,
so he had a fine, quite covetable inheritance.

334   When the father and mother were dead,
relatives came, sad and disheartened;
they told him he should produce some heirs
so that such valuable places would not be left barren.

335   He changed his intent from the one he previously had.
The ways of the world moved him and he said that he
would do it.

---

1. The famous Tuscan city, west of Florence, is on the Arno River, which
flows into the Tyrrhenian Sea, a part of the Mediterranean.

They sought a wife for him who would be suitable,
and they set the day that the wedding would take place.

336   When the day to celebrate the wedding came,
he went with his relatives to take his wife;
he could not attend so well to the Glorious One
as he was wont to do in earlier times.

337   Going down the road to fulfill his pleasure,
he remembered the Glorious One, Whom he had offended;
he considered himself wrong and he held himself as dead,
he pondered this matter that would lead him to a bad port.

338   Reflecting on this matter with a changed heart,
he found a church, a place consecrated to God;
he left the other people outside the portico;
the reformed groom entered to pray.

339   He went into the church, to the most remote corner,
bent his knees, and said his prayer;
the Glorious One full of blessing came to him,
and angrily said these words to him:

340   "You ill-fated, stupid, crazy fool!
What predicament are you in? What have you fallen into?
You seem poisoned, as if you have drunk herbs
or have been touched with Saint Martin's staff.[2]

341   Young man, you were well married to Me;
I very much loved you as a good friend,[3]
but you go around seeking better than wheat bread;[4]
for that reason, you will not be worth more than a fig!

---

2. Saint Martin of Tours (ca. 315-387), patron saint of wine-bibbers and drunkards. To be touched by Saint Martin's staff, then, would be to be drunk.

3. *Amigo*, Spanish: friend, or lover in the sense of "one who loves," a worshipful admirer and devotee.

4. The expression "to seek better than wheat bread" ("buscar mejor de pan de trigo") is proverbial and implies that someone is foolishly involved in a futile endeavor (since there is no bread better than that made of wheat). The phrase is found in the *Libro de Alexandre* (156d): "non quises[s]e buscar me[j]or de pan de trigo" [ed. Dana Nelson (Madrid: Gredos, 1979)]; in Juan Ruiz's *Libro de buen amor* (950d): "Quien mas de pan de trigo busca, syn seso anda" [ed. Julio Cejador y Frauca, 2d ed. (Madrid: Espasa-Calpe, 1960)]; and in Cervantes' *Don Quijote*: "¿No será mejor estarse pacífico en su casa y no irse por el mundo a buscar pan de trastrigo . . .?" [vol. 1, ed. Martín de Riquer (Barcelona: Editorial Juventud, 1965, 78]. Compare *Miracles* 804 (759)c.

342 If you will listen to Me and believe,
     you will not wish to cast aside the first life;[5]
     you will not leave Me in order to have another;
     if you do, you will have to carry firewood on your back!"

343 The chastised groom left the church;
     everyone complained that he had delayed;
     they went on ahead to fulfill their mission,
     the whole business was quickly completed.

344 They had a splendid wedding; and the wife was taken.
     Otherwise, if she had been disdained, it would have been
          an affront.
     The bride was well pleased with this groom,
     but she did not know where the ambush lay.

345 The forementioned man knew well how to cover up;
     his tongue kept his heart's secret;
     he laughed and made merry, all quite appropriately;
     but the vision had him quite disturbed.

346 They had a lavish wedding and very great joy,
     perhaps they never had greater joy in one day;
     but Holy Mary cast Her net around there
     and on dry land made a great catch.

347 When night came, at the time for sleeping,
     they made the newlyweds a bed in which to lie;
     before they had taken any pleasure with each other,
     the arms of the bride had nothing to hold.

348 The husband slipped from her hands, he fled from her;
     no one ever found out where he ended up.
     The Glorious One knew how to keep him well hidden;
     She did not allow him to be corrupted!

349 He left a beautiful woman and very great possessions,
     which very few people would do nowadays;
     they never found out where he was—or was not.
     God bless anyone who does so much for Him!

350 We believe and imagine that this good man
     found some place of great religion,

---

5. The religious life that the young man had promised the Virgin Mary he
would follow.

and hid there to say his prayers,
for which his soul earned a good reward from God.

351   Surely we must believe that the Glorious Mother—
because this man did such a great thing—
would not forget him, for She is merciful;
surely She had him dwell there where She dwells.

The Little Jewish Boy

352 In the city of Bourges, a foreign city,[1]
in another time there occurred a fine deed;
it is told in France and also in Germany,
indeed it is similar and equal to the other miracles.

353 A monk wrote it down, a very truthful man,
he was a monk of the monastery of Sant Miguel de la Clusa.[2]
He was at that time hosteler[3] in Bourges;
Pedro was his name—of that I am certain.

354 In that city, since it was necessary,
a cleric had a school of singing and reading:
he had many pupils learning letters,
sons of good men who wanted to rise in esteem.

355 A little Jewish boy, native of the town, came
for the pleasure of playing with the children;
the others welcomed him, they caused him no grief;
they all took delight in playing with him.

356 On Easter Sunday, very early in the morning,
when the Christian people go to take *Corpus Domini*,
a great desire to commune seized the little Jewish boy:
the woolless lamb took Communion with the others.

357 While they were taking Communion with very great zeal,
the little Jewish boy raised his gaze;

---

1. In central France, today the capital of the department of Cher.

2. This is either Saint-Michel-de-l'Ecluse in Bergerac, Dordogne (France) or San Michele de la Clusa in Susa, Piamonte (Italy).

3. Monk in charge of a hospice maintained by his monastery.

he saw over the altar a lovely figure,
a beautiful Lady with a lovely Child.

358   He saw that this Lady Who was seated
gave Communion to large and small;
he was very pleased with Her, the more he looked at Her
the more he fell in love with Her beauty.

359   He left the church happy and pleased
and went immediately to his house as he was accustomed;
because he was late his father threatened him
saying he deserved to be whipped.

360   "Father," said the boy, "I will not deny anything,
for I was with the little Christians early this morning,
with them I heard Mass splendidly sung,
and with them I partook of the Sacred Host."

361   This grieved the ill-fated man very much,
as if the boy were dead or had had his throat cut;
the bedeviled man in his great wrath did not know what to do;
so he made evil faces like someone demon-possessed.

362   This treacherous dog had inside his house
a large, fierce oven that instilled great terror;
the mad sinner had it fired up
so that it gave off an excessive great heat.

363   The false disbeliever took this little child,
just as he was, shod and clothed,
he threw him in the raging fire.
May ill come to such a father who does such to his son!

364   The mother shouted and clawed herself in despair,
she tore her cheeks with her nails;
many people came in a short time
for they were disturbed by such a loud plaint.

365   The fire, although raging, was very merciful;
it did not harm him one bit, rather it showed him good will;
the little boy escaped from the fire alive and well;
the Almighty King wrought a great miracle!

366   The child lay in peace in the middle of the furnace,
he could not have lain more peacefully in his mother's arms;
he feared the fire no more than he would a young boy
for the Glorious One was giving him company and comfort.

367   He came out of the fire without any injury;
he felt no more heat than at any other time;
he received no marks and no afflictions
for God had bestowed His blessing on him.

368   Everyone asked him, Jews and Christians,
how he was able to conquer such mighty flames
when he did not control his feet or his hands.
Who protected him inside there? Make them certain.

369   The child answered with an outstanding response:
"The Lady Who was in the golden chair,
with Her Son in Her arms, sitting on the altar.
She defended me and I felt nothing."

370   They understood that this was Saint Mary,
that She defended him from such a fierce storm;
they sang great lauds, they had a lavish celebration,
they placed this miracle among the other deeds.

371   They seized the Jew, the false disloyal one,
the one who had done such great wrong to his little son;
they tied his hands with a strong rope
and they cast him into the great fire.

372   In the time it would take for someone to count a few pennies,[4]
he was turned into ashes and embers;
they did not say psalms or prayers for his soul,
rather they hurled insults and great curses.

373   They gave him dreadful rites; they made for him a vile
       offering:
instead of the *Pater Noster*,[5] they said "As he did so may
       he receive."[6]
From this *comunicanda*[7] God defend us,
and let such terrible payment be with the devil.

---

4. The original has "pipiones": A *pipión*, like *dinero*, is a coin of little value.
We translate again "pennies." See also strophes 9d and 324d.

5. Latin for "Our Father," i.e., the first words of the Lord's Prayer, thus the
prayer itself.

6. May he receive his just deserts.

7. A Latinism indicating "Communion" (Dutton *Obras* 2:128). A *comunicanda* is an antiphon sung during Communion, thus the term can be taken
to refer to the service itself.

374   Such is Holy Mary who is full of grace,
for service She gives Glory, for disservice punishment;
to the good She gives wheat, to the evil oats,
the good go to Glory, the others go in chains.

375   Whoever renders Her service is fortunate,
whoever rendered disservice was born in a harsh hour,
the ones gain grace, and the others rancor;
the good and the evil are revealed by their deeds.

376   Those who offend Her or who disserve Her
won mercy if indeed they asked Her for it;
never did She refuse those who loved Her,
nor did She throw in their faces the evil they had done.

377   In order to prove this thing that we have told you,
let us relate a beautiful example that we read;
when it is told, we will believe it better;
we will guard against causing Her grief.

Saint Mary's Church Profaned

378 There were three knights who were friends;
they had a great dislike for another who was their neighbor.
They would have gladly killed him if they could
and sought zealously his cruel death.

379 So much did they discuss and scheme
that one day, when they espied him alone,
they ambushed him, for they intended to kill him;
they wanted that more than great riches.

380 The man understood that they wanted to kill him
and did not dare to face them at all.
He began to flee, for he wanted to escape.
Then they made their move to overtake him.

381 The one who was fearfully fleeing
came upon a church and was greatly delighted;
it was built in honor of the Glorious One;
he hid himself inside it, the wretched sinner.

382 The ones who were following him, who wanted to kill him,
had no respect for the sacred place;
the Glorious One and God abandoned him;
they took his soul from his body.

383 Inside the church consecrated to the Virgin,
this person was mauled and killed.
The Glorious One felt sorely offended;
those who offended Her gained nothing there.

384 The Queen of Glory considered Herself insulted

because Her church was violated;
it weighed heavily on Her heart; She was vexed by it.
She quickly showed them that she was angry with them.

385 God sent upon them an infernal fire;
it did not flame, yet it burned like Saint Martial's fire;[1]
it burned their limbs in a deadly way,
and they cried out loudly: "Holy Mary, help!"

386 With this assault they were badly battered,
they lost feet and hands and wound up deformed,
their legs and arms drawn up to their chests;
Holy Mary was collecting Her due.

387 The people found out about it, and the men did not deny it;
they deserved what they were suffering for it;
they had not considered, when they committed the
sacrilege,
the angry Virtues that now battered them.

388 Neither male nor female saints would help them,
so each day they got worse to the maximum degree;
finally they took the path they should have taken before:
they turned to the Glorious One who was making them burn.

389 They fell in supplication before Her altar,
sobbing as much as they could sob;
they said: "Glorious Mother, deign to pardon us,
for we find no other who can help us.

390 If we deserved harm, dearly have we suffered it;
it will be in our minds as long as we live.
Mother, if You pardon us, we promise
never to use force again in Your church.

391 Mother, You are greatly esteemed for You are merciful;
You always have mercy even when You are angry;
Mother, full of grace, pardon this sin,
give us a good response, tempered and pleasing.

---

1. Saint Martial's fire is the name of a disease also called Saint Anthony's fire. It is a fever ergotism caused by the fungus *claviceps purpurea* which forms on rye, from which the common bread of the poor was made in the Middle Ages. The disease is gangrenous and results in the mortification and loss of limbs. Victims sometimes survive after losing all four limbs.

392 Mother, repentant are we of the error that we committed;
     we erred badly, we committed great madness;
     we took great punishment, we deserved even greater,
     we have paid for the share that we ate.

393 Mother, if You do not help us, we will not part from You;
     if You do not pardon us, we will not depart from this place;
     if You do not succor us, we will consider ourselves nothing;
     without You, we will be unable to put an end to this fever."

394 The Glorious Mother, Solace of the Afflicted,
     did not spurn the moans of the suffering men;
     She did not look at their merits nor at their sins,
     rather She looked to Her temperance and helped the
         burned ones.

395 The Merciful Lady, who was irate before,
     began losing Her wrath and became more mild;
     She delivered them from the wrath that She had raised
         against them;
     all the malady was then abated.

396 The fires that were making them burn died down,
     they had a greater cure than they were wont to have;
     they felt that the Glorious One wanted to favor them;
     they cried with great joy, they did not know what to do.

397 The fires died down; they felt no more pain,
     but never again were they fully masters of their limbs;
     they were forever deformed, forever beggars;
     they always proclaimed themselves as great sinners.

398 With this relief that God wished to grant them,
     they went immediately to the bishop to gain absolution;
     they made confession as they should,
     sobbing loudly, showing great remorse.

399 The bishop instructed them, he heard their confession;
     he knew that they came truly contrite;
     he gave them penance and absolution;
     when all this was done, he gave them his blessing.

400 Besides the many pilgrimages that he ordered them to make,
     and besides the many prayers that he ordered them to pray,
     he ordered them always to carry on their backs
     the weapons that they used to desecrate the church.

401   These penitents, when they had been instructed
and were absolved of all their sins,
departed immediately, sad and dismayed;
they went their separate ways, laden with their weapons.

402   Each went his own way, they did not stay together;
and as for my belief, they never saw each other again;
never again did all three lie under the same roof;
they complied honorably and well with what the bishop
    ordered.

403   If in committing the sin they were indeed reckless,
in doing penance they were very inspired;
their members did not hurt but they went around very
    afflicted,
having bad nights and dark days.

404   If in committing the sin they were blind and stupid,
in correcting it they were steadfast and very devout;
as long as they lived, whether many days or few,
they inflicted on their flesh misery and mortifications.

405   Of the three, one, skinny and very miserable,
came to Amfreville,[2] as the writing says;
he took shelter in the town, they put him up
with a holy woman where he was well lodged.

406   He told the lodgers his entire experience,
how in the church they had gone to excess,
how Holy Mary had been very angry with them,
and how they suffered from the vicious fever.

407   Thinking that what he had said would not be believed,
before many he removed his clothes;
he showed them a sword that he carried hidden,
girded to his flesh with a harsh strap.

408   It was about a half-palm in width;
and near the sword the flesh was very swollen.
That which lay under it was all burned.
The next day he left very early in the morning.

409   The people were all amazed

---

2. Amfreville-sur-Iton, France.

when they heard his powerful story and saw his damaged
    limbs;
wherever they gathered—single or married,
young or old—they all talked of this.

410   This miracle was immediately written and recorded
so that it would not be forgotten.
Many became afraid of committing such a sin,
of desecrating a church or a sacred place.

411   Such is Holy Mary as you can comprehend,
She casts bad nets over those who walk in wickedness;
for believers She does great favors;
many are the examples that you will find of this.

412   The examples are so many that they cannot be counted,
for they increase each day, so say the writings;
these with a hundred others would amount only to a tenth.
May She pray to Christ for the erring people.

❖ MIRACLE 18

The Jews of Toledo

413   In noble Toledo, an archbishop's see,
on a great holy day in the middle of August,
festival of the Glorious One,[1] Mother of the Good Servant,
there occurred a great and very signal miracle.

414   The archbishop, a loyal cleric,
was in the middle of Mass at the sacred altar
with many well-disposed people listening;
the church was full, the choir packed.

415   The very devoted parishioners were in prayer
like people who want to win God's pardon.
They heard a voice of great tribulation
by which the entire procession was upset.

416   A voice from Heaven spoke, pained and angry:
it said, "Hear, Christians, a remarkable thing!
The Jewish people, deaf and blind,
have never been so wicked to Lord Jesus!

417   As the Holy Scriptures tell us,
they committed iniquities against Lord Christ,
that sorrow cut to My heart;
but all their madness had repercussions for them.

418   They felt nothing for the Son who deserved no harm,
nor for His Mother Who saw such affliction.
A people so vile who would do such evil
to such a one as they did, would commit any offense.

---

1. The Day of the Assumption, August 15, when the Virgin Mary was assumed into heaven.

419   Those who in a bad hour were born, false and treacherous,
       are now reviving My former pains.
       They have Me in a tight spot and in a great sweat!
       My Son, Light of Sinners, is on the Cross!

420   They are again crucifying My dear Son.
       Nobody could know how great is My pain!
       A bitter vine sprout is growing in Toledo—
       never was one so wicked nurtured on this earth!"

421   All the clergy heard this voice
       as did many of the laymen in the Mozarab[2] congregation.
       They knew it was the voice of Saint Mary;
       against Her the Jews were making folly.

422   The archbishop, who was singing the Mass, spoke
       and the people who were round about heard him.
       He said: "Believe, O congregation, that the voice that spoke
       is greatly offended and therefore was complaining.

423   Be it known that the Jews are doing something
       against Jesus Christ, Son of the Glorious One.
       Due to this affliction the Mother is displeased;
       thus Her complaint is neither idle nor false.

424   Clergy and laity, all who are gathered here,
       pay attention to this and do not scorn it;
       if you seek this thing out, you will find its trail.
       You will exact justice for this offense.

425   Let us not delay this; let us go to the homes
       of the chief rabbis for we shall find something.
       Let us forego our meal; we will indeed recover it.
       Otherwise, the Glorious One will sorely challenge us."

426   The people and all the clergy moved.
       In great haste they went to the Jewish sector.
       Jesus Christ guided them and so did the Virgin Mary,
       and their treachery was soon discovered.

427   They found in the house of the most honorable rabbi
       a large body of wax shaped like a man.
       It was like Jesus Christ; it was crucified,
       held with large nails, and had a great wound in its side.

---

2. In medieval Spain, the Mozarabs were Christians living in places under Moslem control.

428   What outrage they committed against our Lord.
      There they did it all to our dishonor!
      They executed them immediately, but not with pleasure.
      They got what they deserved, thanks be to the Creator!

429   Those who could be caught were executed.
      They were given a bad meal, which they deserved.
      There they said "*Tu autem*";[3] they received a vile death.
      Afterwards they understood they had committed madness!

430   He who would affront Holy Mary
      should be rewarded as these were rewarded.
      So let us plan to serve and honor Her,
      for Her prayer will aid us in the end.

---

3. *Tu autem*, Latin: the first words of the phrase "*Tu autem Domine, miserere nobis*" which indicates the end of the lesson read during meals in the monastery. Thus, the phrase "they said '*Tu* autem'" means "they came to their end."

❖ MIRACLE 19

The Pregnant Woman
Saved by the Virgin

431 We wish to tell you of another miracle
      that happened in another time in a sea port;
      when you hear it, you will be able to affirm
      the virtue of Mary that is in every place.

432 You will hear in it what the Glorious One is like
      on sea and on land, powerful everywhere,
      how She quickly defends, for She is not lazy
      and never did anyone find such a merciful Mother.

433 Near a salt marsh, Tumba[1] it was called,
      there was an island close to the shore;
      the sea would ebb and flow over it,
      two times a day or sometimes three.

434 Well within the island, very near the waves,
      there was a chapel that was Saint Michael's;
      great miracles always occurred there in that monastery,
      but the entrance was somewhat difficult.

435 When the sea wished to flow out,
      it would do so in a great rush; it could not restrain itself;
      no one, no matter how nimble, could escape it;
      if he did not get out before, he would have to perish there.

436 On the feast day of the precious Archangel[2]

---

1. San Miguel de la Tumba (Mont-Saint-Michel), which is also the setting for Miracle 14.

2. Saint Michael, the Archangel, to whom San Miguel de la Tumba (Mont-Saint-Michel), is dedicated. His feast day is celebrated September 29.

the sea was calmer; it was washing more slowly;
the people heard Mass, and not unhurriedly;
they fled immediately to safety with great speed.

437   One day by chance, with the rest of the congregation,
a frail pregnant woman set out;
she could not protect herself as well on the return
and regretted having entered there.

438   The waves were coming close, the people were at a
            distance;
in her panic her legs became paralyzed;
her companions dared not help her:
in a short time, there were to be many crossings.

439   When they could do nothing else, the people fervently
said in great haste: "Holy Mary, help!"
The helpless pregnant woman, full-fraught with fright,
remained in great trouble among the waves.

440   Those who got out, since they did not see anything,
believed surely without a doubt that she had drowned;
they said: "This poor woman was unfortunate;
her sins laid a cruel ambush for her."

441   When they said this the sea withdrew;
in a short time it returned to its place;
Lord Christ wished to show them a great miracle,
whence they might have something to tell about His Mother.

442   They, all wishing to be on their way,
extended their gaze; they looked toward the sand;
they saw that a lone woman was coming,
with her child in her arms, toward the shore.

443   The people were all amazed,
they thought that fantasy had deceived them;
but in a short time they were assured,
they gave thanks to Christ with all hands uplifted.

444   They said: "Say, lady, for God and charity's sake!
For God's sake we beseech you, tell us the truth!
Tell us all the facts of the matter
and how you were freed from your pregnancy.

445   This thing happened through God, we do not doubt it,
and through Holy Mary to Whom we pray,

and through Saint Michael in whose honor we walk,
this miracle is such that we must indeed write it down!"

446 "Listen," said the woman, "my good company,
I believe that you never heard of a greater deed;
it will be reported throughout foreign lands—
in Greece and in Africa and in all of Spain.

447 When I saw that I could not wrest myself from death,
since I was surrounded by the fierce waves,
I commended myself to Christ and to Holy Mary,
for I knew of no other help for me.

448 While I was in this situation, Holy Mary came;
She covered me with the sleeve of Her cloak;
I felt no more danger than when I slept;
if I lay in a bath I would not be happier!

449 Without care and without affliction, without any pain,
I bore this little son—thanks be to the Creator!
I had a good midwife,[3] there could be none better,
She had mercy on me, a sinner!

450 She granted me a great boon, not single but double:
were it not for Her, I would be drowned;
She aided me in the birth; had She not, I would be hurt.
Never did a woman have such an honored midwife!

451 My situation was just as I tell you:
Holy Mary had great mercy on me,
whence we should all learn a lesson
and beseech Her to free us from the mortal enemy."

452 Everyone received great joy from the miracle;
they gave thanks to God and to Holy Mary;
all the community composed a good canticle,
the clergy could sing it in the church:

453 "Christ, Lord and Father, Redeemer of the World,
Who in order to save the world suffered death and pain,

---

3. Berceo uses the word *madrina* ("godmother" in modern Spanish) here
and in 450d; however, the relationship is between the Virgin Mary and the
pregnant woman (not between the Virgin and the newborn child). Thus,
"midwife" (*partera* or *comadrona* in modern Spanish) seems to be the more
appropriate translation.

blessed be You for You are a good Lord,
never did You feel repugnance for any sinner.

454 You freed Jonah from the belly of the fish,
which held him three days closed up in his stomach;
he received no injury because he was protected by You;
the old miracle today is renewed.

455 The children of Israel obeyed your commandment
and crossed the sea behind Moses;
yet they suffered no harm beneath the waves,
while all their pursuers drowned.

456 The ancient miracles, excellent and honored,
with our own eyes we see them now renewed;
Lord, Your friends in the sea find fords;
the others on dry land find themselves drowned.

457 Lord, Your great and marvellous power,
saved Peter on the perilous sea;
Lord, You Who became incarnate in the Glorious Virgin,
in You alone do we trust and in nothing else.

458 Lord, blessed be Your sacred virtue,
blessed be Your Mother, Crowned Queen,
blessed be You, praised be She,
Lord, in Her You had a blessed abode.

459 Lord, You Who are without end and without beginning,
in Whose hand lie the seas and the wind,
deign to bestow your blessing on this assembly,
that we may all praise you with one will.

460 Men and women—all of us who are here—
we all believe in You and we worship You,
we all glorify You and Your Mother,
let us sing in Your name the 'Te Deum laudamus.'"[4]

---

4. Latin: "We praise you O Lord!" A hymn of thanksgiving.

The Drunk Monk

461   I would like to tell you about another miracle
that happened to a monk of a religious order:
the Devil wanted to frighten him severely,
but the Glorious Mother knew how to impede him.

462   Ever since he was in the order, indeed ever since he was a novice,
he had loved the Glorious One, always doing Her service;
he guarded against craziness, or speaking of fornication,
but he finally fell into vice.

463   He entered the wine cellar by chance one day,
he drank a great deal of wine, this was without moderation.
The crazy man got drunk; he lost his sanity,
until vespers he lay on the hard ground.

464   Then at the hour of vespers, the sun very weak,
he was hardly awake, he walked around dazed.
He went out toward the cloister almost senseless,
everyone understood that he had drunk too much.

465   Although he could not stand up on his feet,
he went to the church as he was accustomed to do;
the Devil tried to trip him up,
because, indeed, he thought to conquer him easily.

466   In the figure of a bull who is raging,
pawing the ground with his hooves, his semblance changed
with fierce horns, angry and irate,
the proven traitor stopped before him.

467   He made bad gestures at him, the devilish thing,
he would put his horns in him, in the middle of his entrails;

the good man was very frightened,
but the Glorious One, Crowned Queen, helped him.

468   Holy Mary came with Her honored garment,
which no living soul could fail to esteem,
She put herself in between him and the Devil,[1]
the oh-so-proud bull was immediately tamed.

469   The Lady threatened him with the skirt of Her mantle,
for him this was a very great punishment,
he fled and went away crying loudly,
the monk remained in peace, thanks be to the Holy Father!

470   A short time later, at a few paces
before he [the monk] began to climb the steps,
he attacked him again with an evil face,
like a dog striking with fangs.

471   It came viciously, teeth bared,
brow very furrowed, eyes open wide[2]
to tear him to pieces, back and sides.
"Wretched sinner," said he, "grave are my sins!"

472   Indeed the monk believed himself to be dismembered,
he was in great affliction, he was badly disturbed,
then the Glorious One helped him, that Gifted One,
as She did to the bull, so She treated the dog.

473   Entering the church on the highest step,
he attacked him again for a third time,
in the form of a lion, a fearsome beast,
bearing ferocity beyond imagination.

474   There the monk believed that he was devoured,
because in truth he saw a grievous encounter,
to him this was worse than all the past ones,
in his mind he cursed the Devil.

475   He said, "Help me Glorious One, Mother, Holy Mary,
may Your grace help me now, on this day,

---

1. Berceo uses the name "Peccado" (Sin) for the devil.

2. We follow Dutton (*Obras* 2:255) in rendering *ojos remellados* as "eyes open wide"; but José Baro (*Glosario*) and Daniel Devoto (ed., *Milagros*) define *remellados* as "bloodshot."

because I am in great danger, I could not be in greater,
Mother do not dwell upon my great madness."

476 Scarcely could the monk complete the words,
Holy Mary came as She was accustomed to come,
with a stick in Her hand to strike the lion,
She put Herself in the middle and began to say,

477 "Sir false traitor, you do not learn a lesson,
but I will give you today what you are asking,
before you go away from here you will pay,
I want you to know with whom you make war."

478 She began to give him great blows,
the big blows drowned out the small,
the lion roared loudly;
he never in his life had his sides so beaten.

479 The Good Lady said to him, "Sir false traitor,
who always walks in evil, you belong to an evil master,
if I ever catch you here in these surroundings,
of what you took today, you will get even worse."

480 The figure faded, it began to flee,
never more did he dare to jeer at the monk,
a long time passed before he could heal.
The Devil was glad when She ordered him to go.

481 The monk who had passed through all this,
was not very recovered from the burden of the wine,
both the wine and the fear had so punished him
that he could not return to his customary bed.

482 The Beautiful Queen of excellent deed
took him by the hand, brought him to his bed,
She covered him with the blanket and the bedspread,
She put the pillow comfortably under his head.

483 Moreover, when She put him in his bed,
She made the sign of the cross over him, he was well
    blessed,
"Friend," She said to him, "rest because you have suffered
    greatly,
as soon as you sleep a little, you will be rested.

484 But this I order you, I tell it to you firmly,
tomorrow morning ask for a certain friend of Mine;

confess yourself to him and you will be in good with Me,
because he is a very good man and will give you good penance.

485   I shall go on my way, to save some other afflicted soul,
that is My pleasure, My customary office,
you remain blessed, commended to God,
but do not forget what I have commanded you."

486   The good man said to her, "Lady, truly
You have shown me great mercy,
and I want to know who You are or what Your name is,
because I will profit from it and You will lose nothing."

487   The Good Lady said, "So you may be well instructed,
I am the One Who bore the true Savior,
Who suffered death and pain to save the world,
to Whom the angels do service and honor."

488   The good man said, "This is believable,
Lady from You this deed could be born.
Lady, let me touch Your feet,
never will I see such great pleasure in this world."

489   The good man insisted, he wanted to get up,
to get on his knees, to kiss Her feet;
but the Glorious Virgin did not want to wait for him,
She withdrew from his sight. He was very sad.

490   He could not see where She had gone,
but he saw great lights shining around Her;
he could not at will take his eyes from Her,
he acted rightly because She had done him great favor.

491   The next morning with the bright light of day,
he looked for the good man as She had commanded him,
he made his confession with a humble face.
He concealed nothing of what had happened.

492   When confession was made, the confessor
gave the monk good advice, he gave him absolution,
Holy Mary put such a blessing on him
that the entire order was worth more because of him.

493   If he was good before, he was from then on better,
he always loved the Holy Queen,

the Mother of the Creator, very much and always did Her
   honor.
He was happy that She welcomed him in Her love.

494   The other good man, I do not know his name,
   the one to whom Holy Mary sent him to learn,
   felt such strong love from loving Her so much
   that he would let his head be cut off for Her.

495   All of the other people, lay and tonsured,
   clerics and canons and monks,
   were all in love with the Glorious One,
   Who knows so well how to help the afflicted.

496   All blessed Her and all praised Her,
   they raised their hands and eyes to Her;
   they told Her deeds, they sang Her laud.
   They spent their days and nights doing this.

497   Gentlefolk and friends, let this deed move us,
   let us all love and praise the Glorious One,
   let us not throw away such a beautiful thing,
   which helps us so much in a dangerous hour.

498   If we will serve Her well, whatever we may ask of Her,
   we will gain it all, let us be very sure;
   let us understand it here long before we die
   that whatever we store there is to our benefit.

499   May She give us Her grace and Her blessing,
   may She keep us from sin and tribulation,
   may She win us remission from our licentiousness,
   so that our souls may not go to perdition.

The Pregnant Abbess

500 Gentlefolk and friends, excellent company,
since God wished to bring you to this place,
should you still like to wait on me a little,
I would like to tell you of another miracle.

501 I would like to tell you of another miracle
that the Glorious One did, Star of the Sea,
if you will hear me, you will indeed swear
that you could not taste a better morsel.

502 In righteous times when truth was valued,
when no one would tell a lie for anything,
back then they lived happily, reached old age,
and in their last years saw their great-grandchildren.

503 God did daily miracles for mankind,
since no one would lie to his Christian neighbor,
the weather was fair, both winter and summer,
it seemed all was simple in the world.

504 If men sinned, they did good penance,
then God pardoned them all ill will,
they placed all their affection in Jesus Christ.
I want to give you a good example of this.

505 I want to tell you a story about an abbess,
who sinned at a propitious time, so it seems to me.
Her nuns tried to slander her,
but they did not harm her worth a bean.

506 In that abbess lay much goodness,
she was very understanding and very charitable,

she guided her convent willingly,
and they lived according to the rules, in all chastity.

507 But the abbess fell one time,
she did something crazy that is strictly forbidden.
She stepped, by chance, on a strongly contaminated weed;[1]
when she looked carefully, she found herself pregnant.

508 Her stomach was growing to her breasts
and freckles were coming out on her cheeks.
Some were big, others smaller,
as in first pregnancies, these little things happen.

509 The affair was understood by her companions;
the lit flame could not be hidden.
It grieved some that she had fallen badly,
but it pleased the others very much.

510 She oppressed them greatly, she held them cloistered,
and she did not consent that they do forbidden things.
They wanted to see her dead, the crazy, unhappy ones;
this happens to superiors sometimes.

511 They saw that it was not something to be covered up,
if so the Devil could laugh at them.
They sent a letter to the bishop to say
that he had not visited them and ought to without delay.

512 The bishop understood in the letter
that either there was a dispute or they had committed
  some folly.
He came to carry out his duty, to visit the convent;
he had to understand the whole business.

513 Let us leave the bishop to rest in his house,
let us leave him at peace to sleep with his household.
And let us tell what the pregnant one did,
for she knew she would be harshly accused the next day.

---

1. Dutton (*Obras* 2:174) explains that this is a folklore image. He refers to Daniel Devoto's article in *Bulletin Hispanique* 59: 12-16, adding that this reference appears in the *romancero* and in traditional poetry in the very Rioja region of Spain where Berceo lived.

514   Near her room where she was accustomed to lodge,
she had a retreat, a convenient place.
It was her oratory where she usually prayed;
the altar was dedicated to the Glorious One.

515   There she had the image of the Holy Queen,
who was health and medicine for all.
She had Her image adorned with a red curtain,
for, in the end, She was Godmother to all.

516   She knew the next day she would be harshly accused,
she had no excuse, it was proven fact.
The fortunate one took good counsel,
it was a marvel, how prudent she was.

517   She entered in her oratory all alone;
(519)[2] she did not ask for any companion.
Then she stopped helpless in first prayer,
but God and her good fortune opened a way for her.

518   She threw herself to the floor before the altar,
(517) she looked at the image, she began to cry.
"Help me," she said, "Glorious One, Star of the Sea,
because I have no other advice that can help me.

519   Mother, we read it well, the scripture says it,
(518) You are of such grace and such great temperance,
that whoever willingly tells You his fear
You immediately help him in all his anxiety.

520   You helped Theophilus[3] who was desperate,
who with his blood made a pact with the Devil.
Through Your good counsel he was reconciled,
whence all mankind gives thanks to You for it.

521   You helped, Lady, the Egyptian,[4]
who was a great sinner because she was a loose woman.
Blessed Lady from whom all good flows,
give me some advice before morning.

---

2. We have adopted the logic of Dutton's reordering of quatrains 517-19 and included the traditional numbers in parentheses.

3. See Miracle 25 (The Miracle of Theophilus).

4. Reference to Saint Mary of Egypt (354?-431?). See Miracle 25, n. 4, for fuller treatment.

522 Blessed Lady, I failed to serve You,
but I always loved to praise and bless You;
Lady, I tell the truth; I do not intend to lie,
I would like to be dead, if I could die.

523 Mother of the King of Glory, Queen of the Heavens,
let flow some medicine from Your grace;
free from a harsh accusation a wretched woman,
this, if You wish it, can be quickly done.

524 Mother, for the love of Your beloved Son,
Son so spotless, so sweet and so perfect,
let not this mercy that I ask of You be denied,
for I see they are pursuing me closely with great shouting.

525 If You do not help me, Lady, with some advice
I am ill-prepared to come to the council;
I want to die here in this little place,
for if I go there they will do me great harm.

526 Crowned Queen, Temple of Chastity,
Fountain of Mercy, Tower of Salvation,
take some pity on this afflicted one,
let Your great pity not run out for me.

527 I want, facing Your Son, to give You as surety,
nevermore will I commit this error.
Mother, if I fail, take such vengeance upon me
that everyone may speak of my disgrace."

528 So earnestly did she say her prayer
that the Mother full of blessings heard her.
Like someone asleep, she saw a great vision,
that ought to bring edification to all.

529 The lady remained asleep from a great weariness,
God worked everything out of His pity.
The Mother of the King of Majesty appeared to her,
two angels of very great brightness with Her.

530 The lady was frightened and greatly terrified,
for she was not accustomed to such a vision.
She was very disturbed by the great brightness,
but she was much relieved of her burden.

531 The Glorious One said to her, "Take courage, abbess,
you are safe with Me, do not complain,

know that I bring you a good promise.
Your prioress would not wish for better.

532   Do not be afraid of falling into censure,
God has kept you from falling into that noose.
Go to them without fear, keep the appointment with
      them;
your back will not be broken because of that."

533   With the solace of the Precious Virgin,
the mother not feeling any pain,
the baby was born, a very beautiful little thing.
The Glorious One sent two angels to take it.

534   She said to the two angels, "I charge you both,
take this little boy to this friend of Mine.
Tell him to rear him for Me, so do I command,
for he will indeed believe you, then return to Me."

535   The two angels moved with great swiftness
and executed the order without delay.
It pleased the hermit more than great riches
because truly it was a great honor.

536   The new mother regained consciousness, crossed herself,
and said, "Help me Glorious One, Crowned Queen!
Is this true or am I deceived?
Blessed Lady, help this sinner!"

537   When she regained consciousness, she touched herself with
      her hands,
on her stomach, her sides and along each loin.
She found her belly limp, her waist very thin
as a woman who is freed from such a thing.

538   In no way could she believe it,
she thought it was a dream, not the real thing.
She felt herself and looked at herself a third time,
finally, assured, she cast doubt away.

539   When the poor pregnant one felt herself delivered,
the sack emptied of the bad flour,
with great joy she began to sing, "Salve Regina,"
the solace and medicine of the afflicted.

540   She wept profusely out of great joy,

and she said beautiful lauds to the Virgin Mary.
She did not fear the bishop nor her sisterhood,
because she was rid of the great malady.

541   She wept profusely, she offered prayers,
she said lauds and blessings to the Glorious One.
She said, "May you be praised, Mother, in all seasons
women and men must always praise You.

542   I was in great care and in great fear,
I fell at Your feet, You gave me courage.
Lady, your good remedy helped me,
You must be praised by all creatures.

543   Mother, I above all ought to bless,
praise, magnify, adore and serve You.
You deigned to save me from such great infamy
for which everyone could always laugh at me.

544   Had this sin of mine gone to the council,
I would be the great joke of all women.
How great and how good is your counsel, Mother,
no one, neither great nor small, could imagine it.

545   For the mercy and the grace that You deigned to grant
          me,
I would not know, Mother, how to thank You,
nor could I ever deserve it, Mother,
but I will never cease giving You thanks."

546   The lady remained in deep contemplation,
praising the Glorious One, saying prayers,
but an order came to her from those convened
that she go to the council to answer the charges.

547   Since she did not fear to fall in discredit,
she went immediately to kneel at the bishop's feet.
She tried to kiss his hands as she should,
but he refused to offer them to her.

548   The bishop began to rebuke her right away;
she had done something for which she must pay.
She should not be an abbess by any means,
nor should she live with other nuns.

549   "All nuns who commit such great dishonesty,

who do not safeguard their bodies or remain chaste,
ought to be thrown out of the order;
Elsewhere, wherever they wish, let them do such dirty
    business."

550 "Lord," she said, "why do you mistreat me?
I am not, thankfully, what you think."
"Lady," said the bishop, "why do you deny it?
You will not be believed for you will be proven guilty."

551 "Lady," said the bishop, "go to the common room,
we will take counsel, afterwards we will do something."
"Lord," said the lady, "do not say anything bad,
I commend myself to God, Who can and does protect."

552 The abbess went out of the assembly,
as the bishop ordered, she went to the living quarters.
Anger and hatred had their meeting,
they kneaded their dough with barley flour.[5]

553 The bishop said to them, "Friends, we cannot
condemn this lady unless we prove it."
The convent said to him, "Given what we know well,
lord, why shall we enter into another proof?"

554 The bishop said to them, "When she is convicted,
you will be safer, she more ashamed.
Otherwise, our judgment would be reproached,
after all she cannot be exonerated."

555 He sent his clerics, in whom he trusted most,
so that they might prove how it was.
They took off her skirt although it grieved her.
They found her so thin that she looked like a board.

556 They did not find on her any sign of pregnancy,
neither milk nor trace of any evil-doing.
They said, "This is nothing but a great illusion,
Never was there proffered such an extraordinary lie."

557 They returned to the bishop, they said to him, "Lord,

5. The metaphor of the barley dough ("massa de farina de ordio") is in keeping with the hierarchy of bread and grains which Berceo has established. In
this hierarchy, wheat is the grain *par excellence* and the others (oats and
barley) decidedly inferior. Compare strophes 137, 274, and 374.

know that the sister is blamed in vain;
whoever tells you something else, saving your honor,
tells you so great a lie; there could be none greater."

558 The bishop thought they were deceived,
that the lady had promised them money.
He said, "Evil men, you are not to be believed,
because she is keeping something hidden under wraps."[6]

559 He said, "I will not believe you so quickly,
either you are embarrassed or you took money.
I want to see this with my own eyes,
if it is not so, those who made the accusation must suffer
for it."

560 The bishop got up from where he was seated,
went to the abbess, angry and irate,
made her, against her will, take off her habit,
and found they denounced her for a crime falsely proven.

561 He returned to the convent, angry and very violent.
"Sisters," he said, "you committed a great treachery;
you said such evil about this woman
that your religious order is greatly demeaned.

562 This cannot pass without justice,
the blame you tried to cast on her,
the *Decretum*[7] orders must fall on you;
you must be thrown out of this place."

563 The abbess saw the sisters judged badly,
that they were to be expelled from the house.
She took the bishop aside, a good fifteen paces,
"Lord," she said, "the ladies are not very guilty."

564 She told him her business, why it had happened,
how she was deceived, of her grave sins,

---

6. "She is keeping something hidden under wraps" captures the intent of
Berceo's "otra quilma tiene de yuso los vestidos" ("she has another sack
under her clothes").

7. The *Decretum* is a reference to *Decretum Gratiani* (*Gracian's Decree*),
which was written with the title *Concordia discordantium canonum* (*A
Harmony of Conflicting Canons*). The work appeared in 1140 and soon became the standard text for teaching canon law. Its author Gracian is believed to have been a teacher of canon law at Bologna.

and how the Crowned Virgin helped her.
Were it not for Her, she would be badly censured.

565 And how She ordered the child carried off,
how She ordered the hermit to rear him,
"Lord, if you wish you can prove it,
for charity's sake, let not the sisters lose their place.

566 I would rather be shamed alone
than see so many good nuns cast out.
Lord, I ask you for mercy, pardon this time,
may the penance for all be given to me."

567 The bishop was amazed, he changed color,
he said, "Lady, if this can be proven,
I will see that Lord Jesus Christ is pleased with you;
as long as I live, I will do your bidding."

568 Then he sent two canons to the hermit,
to prove if this was truth or deceit.
They found the good man in a strange habit,
holding the little boy wrapped in a cloth.

569 He showed them the infant newly born that day,
and said that Holy Mary ordered that he be reared.
Whoever might doubt this, would commit a great folly,
since it was the pure truth and not a barefaced lie.

570 They returned immediately to the bishop with the
        message,
they told him the news of what they had proven.
"Lord," they said, "be assured of this,
if not, you will commit a great error, you will acquire
        great sin."

571 The bishop considered himself mistaken regarding the
        abbess,
he fell to the floor, prostrate, at her feet.
"Lady," he said, "have mercy for I have greatly sinned,
I pray that my sin may be pardoned by you."

572 "Lord," said she, "for God and the Glorious One,
consider your position, do not do such a thing.
You are a holy man, I, a grievous sinner,
if you do not return to your feet, I will be angry with you."

573   The abbess had this argument with the bishop,
but they ended completely in good agreement.
Forever they had both love and good will,
they cloistered their lives with great patience.

574   The bishop established peace in the convent,
he ended the disagreement and dissension.
When he wanted to take leave, he gave them his
     benediction;
the visit was good for one and all.

575   He sent his greeting to the holy hermit,
as to a good friend, to a baptismal godfather,
that he rear the child until his seventh year.
Then he would strive to make him a good Christian.

576   When the term came, seven years had passed,
he sent two of the most honored of his clerics
to bring the child from the forest to the town.
They fulfilled the mission as persons well instructed.

577   They brought the child, reared in the wilderness.
For his age, he was well-taught;
it pleased the bishop, he was very satisfied.
He ordered him to study with a learned teacher.

578   He turned out a very good man, temperate in
     everything;
it seemed indeed that he was reared by a good master.
The whole town was very pleased with him
and when the bishop died, they gave him the bishopric.

579   The Glorious One, who had given him to be reared, guided
     him.
With God, he knew how to govern his bishopric well;
he guided the souls well, as he should.
In all things he knew how to seek moderation.

580   The people loved him as did his clergy;
the canons and all the nuns loved him.
Everyone, wherever they were, prayed for his days,
except some crazy ones who loved folly.

581   When the time came for him to die,
his Lady did not let him suffer long.

She carried him to Heaven, to a safe place,
where neither thief nor judge[8] can ever enter.

582 We all give thanks to the Glorious Virgin,
of Whom we read and prove so many miracles.
May She give us grace so that we may serve Her,
and guide us to do things for which we may be saved.
(Amen).

---

8. Berceo expresses an intense distrust of judges (*merinos*). See Dutton's
remarks in his edition (*Obras* 2:171) and in his article in *Bulletin of Hispanic Studies* 37 (1960):137-45 for an explanation of this dislike.

The Shipwrecked Pilgrim Saved by the Virgin

583   Gentlefolk, if you wish, while daylight lasts,
I will tell you even more of these miracles;
if you do not complain, I will not complain,
because Holy Mary is like a deep well.

584   Holy Mary is like a mighty river,
that everyone drinks from, beasts and people,
it is as great tomorrow as it was yesterday, and it is never
    empty,
it runs in all seasons, in hot and in cold.

585   She always helps in all places,
in valleys and mountains, on lands and seas;
those who know how to pray to Her with a pure mouth,
will not suffer severe pain in their loins.

586   We read a miracle of Her Holiness
that happened to a bishop, a man of charity;
a Catholic man of great authority,
he saw it with his own eyes, certainly he knew the truth.

587   Just as he saw it, so he wrote it,
he omitted nothing, nor did he add to it,
may God grant him paradise for he surely deserved it,
he said no mass that helped him so much.

588   Some pilgrims went on a crusade to the Holy Land,
to salute the sepulchre, to pray to the true cross;
they embarked on ships to go to Acre,
if the Heavenly Father wished to guide them.

589   They had favorable winds immediately at the beginning,
       a very delightful breeze, the whole sea tranquil;
       the happy crowd was very joyful,
       with such weather they would have crossed the sea
          quickly.

590   They had passed over a great part of the sea,
       they would have passed the other part quickly,
       but their destiny held for them a bad trap,
       great joy was turned into sadness.

591   The storm moved in, a fierce wind,
       the pilot who guided the ship lost his wits;
       he gave no command, neither to himself nor to others,
       all of his skill was not worth one bean.

592   Another thing happened to them, a grievous harm:
       the ship broke apart down in its depths,
       they saw much water gush in, breaking into every corner,
       everything was going to ruin.

593   Near the big ship they had a smaller one,
       I do not know whether they call it a galley or a pinnace,
       so that if they were worried about a bad wind,
       in that small one they might escape the grave danger.

594   The captain, as would a loyal Christian,
       took the lord bishop by the hand.
       And put him, with other good men of very important
          status,
       in the boat; he followed good advice.

595   One of the pilgrims thinking he was wiser,
       jumped from the ship because he was very agile;
       he intended to enter the galley as a shipmate,
       he drowned in the water; he died but not alone.

596   A half-hour could barely have passed,
       God wished it to happen, the ship was sunk;
       of the people who had remained inside,
       none escaped alive.

597   The bishop and the others who got out with him,
       went to the closest land they could;
       they made a great moaning for those who had perished;
       it grieved them because they had not died with them.

598   Having great affliction and grief for the dead,
        they looked out afar, they looked at the sea,
        in case they might see some of the dead reach shore,
        since the sea never wants to hide dead things.

599   Looking to see if they could spot some of the dead,
        to bury them, to put them in the ground,
        they saw little doves born from under the sea,
        as many as the dead so many could they be.

600   They saw little doves come out from under the sea,
        flying whiter than snow against the sky;
        they believed they were the souls God wanted to carry
        to holy Paradise, a glorious place.

601   With righteous envy, they were beside themselves
        they were sorely grieved that they were alive,
        since they believed very firmly, there was no doubting
        that the doves were the souls of those the sea swallowed.

602   They said, "Alas, pilgrims! You were lucky,
        you are now passed through fire and through water;
        we remain in the wilderness as helpless ones,
        we keep vigil so that you may rest in peace.

603   Thanks to the Holy Father and to Holy Mary,
        you now wear the palm of your pilgrimage;[1]
        we are in sadness and you in joy,
        we intended to do a good thing and we committed folly."

604   Having great grief from the harm that came to them,
        they wanted to go on, to start their journey;
        they saw a traveler come out of the sea,
        it seemed that he was a wretched pilgrim.

605   When he came to them, it was on the shore,
        all knew him, he was the one who had jumped,
        they all crossed themselves, "How, in what way
        did he remain alive in the sea one whole hour?"

606   The pilgrim said, "Hear me, and live!
        I will make you believe what you doubt,
        I want you to know how I escaped alive,
        you will say 'Thanks be to God' as soon as you hear it.

---

1. The palm is the reward of martyrdom and symbol of the same.

607 When I tried to jump out of the big ship,
  for it was clear it was going to sink,
  I saw I could not save myself from death;
  I began to say, 'Help me, Holy Mary!'

608 I said these words, 'Help me, Holy Mary!'
  I could not say more for there was no time;
  She was instantly ready, since it pleased Her;
  if it were not for Her, I would be drowned.

609 She was swift, She brought a good cloth,
  it was a cloth of value, never did I see its equal;
  She threw it over me, She said, 'No harm will come to
   you;
  believe that you fell asleep or lay in a bath.'

610 Never did a man of flesh see such exquisite work,
  it was the work of angels rather than material;
  I lay as comfortable as if under a tent,
  or as someone who falls asleep in a green meadow.

611 Happy will be the soul and fortunate
  that under such an exquisite cover is solaced;
  neither cold nor heat nor wind nor ice
  will vex it to annoyance.

612 Under this cloth they rest, happy and satisfied,
  the glorious virgins, beloved of Lord Christ,
  who sing multiple lauds to His Mother,
  and have beautiful and honorable crowns.

613 The shade of that cloth is so soothing
  that one who is hot finds coolness beneath it,
  and one who is cold finds tempered warmth;
  God, what magnificent help in times of anguish!'[2]

614 So many are Her rewards, so many Her charities,
  so many Her virtues, so many Her blessings,
  that neither bishop nor abbot could count them,
  nor could kings nor very rich men imagine them.

615 The grief that those in danger had,
  they forgot it all with the pleasure of the miracle;

---

2. The Virgin causes a cloth to capture and hold a thief in Miracle 24 ("The Robbed Church").

they rendered thanks to God, they chanted the "Te Deum,"
then they finished sweetly with "Salve Regina."

616   The pilgrims then completed their pilgrimage;
they arrived at the sepulchre with very great joy,
they adored the Cross of the Son of Mary,
never in this world did they see such a good day.

617   They told of the miracle of the Glorious Mother,
how She freed the man from the perilous sea;
they all said it was a wondrous thing,
they had a delightful story written about it.

618   However many heard this holy miracle,
they all repeated the prayers to the Glorious One,
they had better devotion in serving Her,
since from Her they hoped for mercy and reward.

619   The fame of this deed flew over the seas,
the wind did not stop it, it dwelt in many homes;
they put it in books in many places,
where it is praised by many mouths today.

620   As many as bless the Glorious Mother,
by the King of Glory, do the right thing!
since through Her we come out of the harsh prison,
the dangerous abyss in which we all lie.

621   We, who because of Eve, have fallen into damnation,
through Her we recover our lost paradise;
were it not for Her, we would lie dead,
but Her Holy Fruit has redeemed us.

622   Through Her Holy Fruit that She conceived,
He who suffered passion and death for the world's salvation,
we come out of the pit that Adam opened for us,
when, against the proscribed evil, he took a bite.

623   Since then She always strives to help the afflicted,
to guide the wretched, to call back the sinner,
on land and sea She does great miracles,
such and even greater ones than those that are told.

624   May She, Who is abundant and full of grace,
guide our actions, our sad lives;
may She, in this world, guard us from treacherous attack,
and in the other, win for us a dwelling with the saints. (Amen).

The Merchant of Byzantium

625 Friends, if you would like to pay a little heed,
I would read a beautiful miracle to you;
when it has been read, you will be very pleased,
you will prize it more than an average meal.

626 In the city that is named for Constantine,
since Constantine founded it in earlier times,
he who gave Rome to Saint Peter as a home,
there was a good man of great estate.

627 This burgher had a very good heart,
in order to increase his fame, he made great expenditures;
he spent his fortune, he gave it freely,
no matter who asked him, he would not say no.

628 To enhance his reputation, to increase his esteem,
he shared without regret, all the money he could;
if his own dwindled, to gain still greater fame,
he willingly borrowed from his neighbors.

629 He spent his wealth generously and without prudence,
his riches grew smaller but not his good will;
one always would find people in his house,
at times twenty, thirty, sometimes a hundred.

630 Since he made great expenditures, spending without
moderation,
his money gave out, and he found himself in great need;
he did not find a loan, nor did he find usury,
either among strangers or among his acquaintances.

631 Everyone understood that he was impoverished,
he found no loan nor did he have credit;
the good man had fallen into great difficulty;
he considered the past all lost.

632 The man with great complaint went before the altars,
he uttered his prayers aloud:
"Lord who art one God and three equal persons,
be merciful and do not abandon me.

633 Lord, until now, You have sustained me,
now, due to my sins, I have fallen in need;
I have lost all the esteem I had;
it would have been better had I not been born.

634 Lord, give me advice in some way,
send me Your grace by some path;
for You, such an act is a very easy thing.
I swam the whole sea, will I die on the shore?"

635 While he was praying, God wished to help him.
The burgher thought of a good recourse;
it did not come from his own head, rather
the One Who rules the world wished to guide him.

636 There was in the city a very rich Jew,
there was no richer man in that vicinity;
he decided to go to him
to ask his advice for God and charity's sake.

637 Then he went to the Jew and was well received,
the Jew asked him how he was and why he had come,
for he had known him in other times
and had indeed heard all his concerns.

638 The burgher told the Hebrew his business,
"Sir, I believe that you indeed know my situation;
I would like very much to obtain a loan from you,
since I never thought I would see myself in this predicament.

639 When God willed me to have wealth,
as my neighbors know, I helped everyone;
I had the doors of my house open,
whatever God gave me, I shared with all.

640 I would like, if I could, to continue doing that,
but I am very downhearted and diminished in riches;

but if you would give me credit from yours,
I will return it to you at a fixed time."

641 The Jew said to him, "I will gladly do it,
I will lend you however much you want of my wealth,
but give me a guarantor so that I may be certain;
if you do not, I would fear being deceived."

642 The Christian said to him, he spoke to him wisely:
"Sir, I cannot give you any other guarantor,
but I will give you Christ, my God and my Lord,
Son of the Glorious One, Savior of the world."

643 The Jew said to him, "I could not believe
that He of Whom you speak, born of Mary,
is God, but that He was a sane man and not mad,
a true prophet; I would not believe anything else.

644 If he will be your surety, I, for His love,
will give you a loan without any other guarantor,
but it seems to me a despicable, vain thing,
and you seem to me almost a mocking man.

645 I do not know how He could guarantee the loan
because He is not in this world, as I believe;
do not hope that He is coming to help you,
whence it behooves you to get other counsel."

646 The Christian answered him, he said to the Jew,
"I understand that you consider me mad and foolish,
that I do not have sense and that I am a fool,
but I trust after this you will see otherwise."

647 The Jew said to him, "If you demonstrate such a thing,
I will give you the loan, however much you ask,
but if this is a trick, with what you get from me
you will not be paying either singers or minstrels."

648 The burgher said to the renegade rogue,
"Just come with me to my shrine;
I will show you Mary with Her Good Son."
The Jew said to him, "I will do it gladly."

649 He took him to the church; with God and His guidance,
he showed him the image of Holy Mary,
with Her Son in Her arms, Her Sweet Companion.
Those of the Jewish quarter were ashamed.

650 The good man said to those of the synagogue,
"This is our Lord and this our Lady,
whosoever calls on Them is always very fortunate;
whosoever does not believe in Them will drink fire and
flames."

651 He said to the Jew who was the most respected,
the one who promised to lend him money,
"These are my Lords and I their servant,
let These be my surety for I can offer nothing else."

652 The Jew said to him, "Then I will take Them,
I will not ask you for other guarantors;
but if you fail me, I will challenge Them,
and I will make known what kind of loyalty you bring."

653 The Christian gave the Guarantors to the rogue,
he put in his hand Mother and Son;
they agreed on a certain date for his payment,
the citizen burgher received the money.

654 When the citizen had received the money,
he was joyous and considered himself saved,
he returned to the Glorious One, he went there with good
conscience,
he went to give thanks to God with all his heart.

655 He bent his knees before the Majesty,
he raised his eyes to God with great humility;
"Lord," he said, "You were merciful and charitable to me;
You have taken me out of great poverty today.

656 Lord, yesterday I was poor and in debt,
today, because of Your Grace, I am rich and in
abundance;
I gave You for a guarantor, but I did it unwillingly;
it would be a grievous error if You were challenged because
of me.

657 Lord, I would not want my word to fail;
what I propose to You I want to fulfill it,
but if I cannot come on the appointed day,
I will send the money to You.

658 Lord, if by chance I am far away,
so I cannot come at the time agreed,

I will put before You, what You have guaranteed for me,
and You, however You wish, pay him in full.

659   Queen of Heaven, Mother of wheat bread,[1]
by whom the mortal enemy was beaten,
You are my surety, I say the same thing to You,
that I have told to the One You have with You."

660   When the burgher had said his prayer,
and had placed his contract with the rogue,
he arranged his affairs and readied his departure;
he went to foreign lands, to a distant region.

661   He went to foreign lands, to Flanders and France,
with much merchandise and he made great profit;
with God and the Glorious One his worth grew,
he rose to great wealth and great excellence.

662   With the large business in which he was occupied,
he was very distant from his country;
he did not return on the agreed day,
due to his grave sins, he had forgotten it.

663   The day that he was to pay was approaching;
only one day more was to pass;
the burgher remembered the business;
the good man wanted to kill himself with his own hands.

664   He said, "I have failed badly, wretched sinner,
I cannot help the guarantor at all,
my Redeemer will be challenged because of me,
and His Holy Mother, She of Rocamadour.[2]

665   Lord, you understand and you know the truth,
how very grieved I am in my heart;
Lord, give me advice for pity's sake,
so that Your Great Majesty may not be challenged."

---

1. The wheat bread is the best and from it the host is made. Therefore, the
pan de trigo, or wheat bread, is Christ. See Dutton (*Obras* 2:196) and Mount
(Levels).

2. The image of the Virgin of Rocamadour (Lot, France) was highly revered
in the Middle Ages and the chapel that held it was an important pilgrimage
destination. According to legend, the image was carved by Zaccheus the
Publican, who went from the Holy Land to France, where he lived as
Amadour.

666 He took all the money, tied in a sack,
not a worn-out *penny*³ was missing;
he brought it to the shore, carried on his back;
he threw it into the waves where there was no ford.

667 He turned to Jesus Christ with great devotion,
crying hard he said his prayer,
"Lord," he said, "You know this whole matter,
because You are the Guarantor of our agreement.

668 Lord, since I cannot pay the moneylender,
because between us there lies a very rough path,
Lord, Who art called the true Savior,
put this money in his coffer tomorrow.

669 Glorious Lady, my Holy Mary,
You indeed are in the midst of this business;
when You look at it carefully, it is Yours more than mine,
I give You the money, Lady, You guide it.

670 Both You and Your Son were in the agreement,
You are both Guarantors to the renegade rogue;
let it be Your will that he be paid tomorrow;
by a bad servant let not the Good Lord be challenged.

671 I entrust it to You, I consider that I have paid,
I hold myself as free because I have given it to You;
I, Mother, pray to You, You beseech Your Son;
however You wish, tomorrow let the rogue be paid."

672 It pleased the Glorious One, also Her Beloved Son;
the next day in the morning with the bright sun,
the chest carrying the money on loan,
floated to the door of the infidel rogue.

673 The town where the Jew had his home,
the one who had lent the burgher the money,
lay inhabited, so we read, near the sea,
the waves sometimes beat against its walls.

674 On that morning, at almost the hour of prime,
those of the Jewish quarter, a useless lot,
went to entertain themselves on the shore;
they saw this box floating near the beach.

---

3. The *pugés* (here translated as "penny") is a coin of infinitesimal value of the archbishopric of Puy.

675 They went to catch it, frivolous youths,
these who many times make vain attempts;
it slipped away and escaped their hands;
many people saw this, Jews and Christians.

676 Some wise Christians came at the noise,
with grapples, hooked poles, swift boats;
nothing at all helped since they were all knaves,
never did men exude more useless sweat.

677 By chance the true owner came by,
the chest came to his hands right away;
he carried it to his house, inside in his larder,
he made a great pile of gold and silver.

678 When the rogue had put away the money,
the chest that it came in was carefully examined;
he put it under his bed greatly lightened;
everyone was envious of the renegade rogue.

679 The treacherous rogue, greedy by nature,
(he who is vile thinks of nothing else)
considered that his good fortune was marvelous;
he called the burgher "liar."

680 The Jews, those ill-tempered ones, reproached him
for he had lost his money due to his very madness;
never had any one accepted so senseless a surety
as to take as guarantor a hard statue.

681 Let us leave the Jew, greedy and usurious.
Let God not take him out of there; let him guard his larder.
Let us talk instead about the merchant's affairs;
let us bring him the news of where the chest made shore.

682 The burgher of Byzantium lived in great grief,
for he could not pay the Jew at the appointed time.
The good man could not brighten his face;
his men could not comfort him no matter what.

683 A long time passed, he earned a great deal of money,
buying and selling according to the law of merchants;
when the time came he left those paths,
he returned to his province with other companions.

684 He went to Constantinople, the news went round,
that the burgher, Sir Valerio, had come.

It pleased the Jew, he considered himself lucky;
he thought he would double the money lent.

685 He went straight to the merchant's house; he knew where
  he lived.
The Jew insulted him because he had not paid;
the good man told him he must be mad,
for nothing of what he was claiming did he owe him.

686 The Jew said to him, "I am in the right
for I have good witnesses for what I ask of you.
If you say you paid, show the where and the when,
but in the end I believe I will not come out singing.

687 I trusted in your Christ, a great trickster,
and in His Little Mother Who was scarcely better.
I will get such satisfaction as the guarantor I took;
whoever so trusts you, may he receive the same."

688 The Christian said to him, "You are speaking wildly,
Good Mother, Good Son, you have little respect for
  Them;
never in this world did a wimple cover such a Lady,
nor was a child ever born with such gifted speech.

689 The money you gave me, I am very certain,
for I have good witnesses, I have repaid you.
If you still say no, I will make you a better offer:
let the Guarantors say what you have taken."

690 The rogue was happy, he considered himself protected,
he said, "I am in agreement and defer to your rebuttal."
He thought that the image had no feeling
and could not say a word that might convict.

691 They went to the church, these two contestants,
to make the inquiry regarding who had the money.
Many went behind them and many in front,
to see if the wooden figures would have the ability to speak.

692 They stopped before the Crowned Child,
Whom the Mother sweetly embraced.
The citizen said to Him, "Lord so perfect,
judge this suit for I am sorely challenged.

693 You are informed of how I did it,
whether he received it or not, you know it, Lord.

Lord, shed Your grace over me, sinner;
say whether he received it, since You were the Guarantor."

694   The Crucifix spoke, it told him a good lesson,
"You lie because you received payment on the designated day:
the basket in which the carefully counted money came,
you have hidden under your own bed."

695   The whole town went, as it wished;
they went to the house, they were quite correct to do so.
They found the chest where it lay under the bed;
the evil rogue was confused and in a sorry state.

696   Sad and fearful, like it or not,
he had to tell the whole business.
He and his companions were immediately converted;
he died in the good faith, wrested from sin.

697   Always on that day that this thing happened,
when the image spoke, due to its excellent virtue,
they hold a noble festival with hymns and poems,
with great exultations to God and to the Glorious One.

698   The people of the town, paupers and wealthy,
all rejoiced with instruments;
they prepared banquets, they gave to those who had not
their own salted and fresh meat and fish.

699   The glasses of strong wine went round,
marvelously prepared dishes;
whoever wanted to partake need not do without;
they did not feel any scorn at this time.

700   A rich archdeacon, from very foreign lands,
happened on this feast among that company;
he saw great dances, huge processions
the likes of which he had never heard nor seen.

701   He asked how this festival was started,
for it was a great event, nobly celebrated.
A Christian told him of its much discussed origin,
and he knew that this was a proven truth.

702   It pleased the archdeacon who considered it a great event;
he said, "May God and the Glorious Virgin be praised!"
He put it in writing with his fine script.
May God grant him paradise and delightful rest. (Amen).

❖ MIRACLE 24 (25)

The Robbed Church

703   I would like to tell you of yet another miracle
(867)[1] that the Glorious One did. She is not to be forgotten.
       She is a perennial fountain from which the sea is fed,
       which in all seasons never ceases to flow.

704   Indeed I believe that whoever hears this miracle
(868) will not want to take off the wimple that covers her,
       or snatch away by force what she holds.
       This must be remembered as long as you live.

705   This very beautiful miracle happened
(869) in the time of the King of good fortune,
       Don Fernando by name,[2] Lord of Extremadura,
       grandson of King Alfonso, a person of great temperance.

706   Thieves left from around Leon,
(870) from the bishopric of that region.
       They came to Castile in great confusion
       led by the Devil, who is a wicked guide.

707   One was a layman born in a bad hour;
(871) the other a cleric ordained by the bishop.
       They arrived in Çohinos. The Devil led them,
       the one who directed Judas in his evil negotiation.

---

1. As indicated in the introduction to the translation, we have followed Dutton's suggestion for reversing the traditional order of Miracles 24 and 25. This requires renumbering the quatrains in each miracle tale as well. The traditional numbers for the tales themselves and for their quatrains are given in parentheses.

2. This is Fernando III el Santo, grandson of Alfonso VIII, who died in 1252. This reference sets the tale in the time of Berceo.

708   Outside the town, in a plain
(872) not very far away, there was a church.
      Near the church, there was an inhabited convent.
      A Dominican nun lived therein.

709   They spied out the place both of these thieves.
(873) They moved by night each one with a pickaxe.
      They unhinged the doors and looked in the corners.
      They discerned that indeed the convent was without men.

710   The nun was poor who kept the hermitage.
(874) She had little food, very few clothes,
      but she had a cloth, which was very good.
      For a woman of the order, it was a seemly covering.

711   What was in the convent was all emptied out,
(875) badly handled, placed in a sack.
      The layman was a man of a rather bad conscience,
      but worse was the cleric, who had read more.

712   When the contents of the convent were added together,
(876) it would all be worth very little in money.
      The miserable ones, ministers of the Devil,
      believed that everything valuable was in the locked
        church.

713   With the pickaxes the lock was yanked off;
(877) the doors unhinged; the church robbed.
      Nothing remained of what was there.
      They did a great sacrilege for a very slight gain.

714   They stripped the cloths that covered the altar,
(878) the vestments and books with which they [the clergy]
        would chant.
      The precious place, where sinners would pray
      to the Creator, was badly damaged.

715   After doing this great madness,
(879) they both raised their faces upward.
      They saw the image of the Glorious Virgin
      with her Child in arms, her Sweet Infant.

716   She had a most honored crown on her head,
(880) covered with a white and very sheer wimple.
      To the left and right she had it beautifully draped.
      They intended to take it from her, but did not profit at all.

717   The cleric hurried and became more daring,
(881) for in ecclesiastic things he was more versed.
      He went to snatch the wimple, the unfortunate man,
      since with that action they would have their business
        finished.

718   The Glorious One considered herself dishonored,
(882) since they had despoiled her so villainously.
      She showed that she was not very pleased with the service.
      Never did anyone see a wimple so lamented.

719   As soon as the evildoer snatched the wimple,
(883) it stuck to him so firmly on his closed fist
      that it would not be so stuck with glue,
      or with a nail driven by a hammer.

720   They lost memory since they well deserved to;
(884) the layman and the cleric lost all their wits.
      They went for the door. They could not find it,
      those born for evil, went wandering in circles.

721   They could not let loose of what they had taken.
(885) Now they wanted, willingly, to leave it if they could.
      They would leave it with pleasure. They did not wish to
        carry it off,
      but they did not know how to judge where the door was.

722   They went groping from corner to corner
(886) as Sisinnio[3] did, the jealous man,
      husband of Teodora, a woman of great song,
      who was converted by Pope Clemens.

723   The mad star-crossed ones, abandoned by God,
(887) were going around like drunkards all dazed.
      Now they fell on their faces, now on their sides.
      They were badly prepared to go on a pilgrimage.

---

3. Saint Clement, pope and martyr of the first century, converted a Roman lady, Theodora, wife of Sisinio, to Christianity. One day Sisinio and his servants followed his wife to the church where she heard Saint Clement say mass. They lost their sight and hearing when they tried to leave, but the prayers of Theodora and Saint Clement restored their senses and Sisinio was converted. This information is given by Michael Gerli in his edition of the *Milagros de Nuestra Señora* (190). See also Daniel Devoto "Notas al texto" 23-25.

724 The anchoress, with the loss she had suffered,
(888) came out as best she could from where she had lain hidden.
She started to shout and call out and she was soon helped.
The fastest people came immediately.

725 Then a great crowd of people came.
(889) They entered the church and found the thieves.
Then they attacked them as the felons emerged,
giving them hard blows with very big sticks.

726 They hit them with great sticks and great blows to the face,
(890) and many numerous kicks and many blows with crossbars.
They raised so many great welts on their bodies
that the small ones were forgotten.

727 They made them tell the whole case;
(891) from what land they came or for what pilgrimage,
and how Holy Mary had caught them,
because they had done Her a great villainy.

728 Before dawn they were well imprisoned;
(892) when the sun rose it found them well tamed.
Everyone called them proven traitors,
who against the Glorious Lady were so fearlessly daring.

729 After Mass was said, the council met.
(893) All felt like doing a bad deed to them.
They made a bad decision concerning the evil layman.
They raised him from the ground with a strong cord.

730 When a devout canon who led a very holy life,
(894) and had his love well kindled in God,
saw the wimple sewed to the hand,
he said that such justice was unheard of.

731 The good man wished to take the wimple,
(895) kissing the veil instead of the Glorious Lady,
but God wanted to honor the good Christian,
and He unstuck the wimple right then from the thumb.

732 A few days later, as God wished to guide him,
(896) it happened that the bishop came to the place.
They led the cleric to introduce him to the bishop,
to see whether he would order the cleric held or freed.

733 They led the cleric with hands well tied,
(897) his shoulders severely thrashed with crossbar blows.

They told him the news of his late night deeds,
and how he did the things that God had forbidden.

734   He himself confessed with his own mouth,
(898)   his whole case, his crazy way of maintaining himself.
How they had stolen the wimple from the Glorious Lady;
never did they do anything of such little profit.

735   The bishop took him and brought him to Leon,
(899)   hands tied behind according to the law for a thief.
Whoever saw him and knew the reason
said, "May God shame him, such a crazy man!"

736   The bishop did not dare to judge the case.
(900)   He called all the clergy to council.
When they had arrived on the assigned day,
he presented the cleric to them and told them of his
     madness.

737   He asked them for advice. What should be done with him?
(901)   No one knew how to respond to that.
The bishop indeed knew how to interpret the law.
He wanted to put blame on the cleric by his (own)
     admission.

738   The bishop said, "Cleric, did you do such evil?
(902)   Do you admit to what they accuse you of?"
"Sir," said the cleric, "my spiritual father,
for my evil deed I never found a match.

739   However much they tell you of me, all is very true.
(903)   They do not tell you a tenth of my wickedness.
Sir, for God's sake and for charity,
do not consider my merit, but rather your goodness."

740   "Friends," said the bishop, "this is appropriate,
(904)   he is not our cleric or of our bishopric.
It is not legitimate that he be condemned by us.
Let his bishop judge him: his merit, his sin.[4]

741   He declares himself to be claimed by the bishop of Avila.
(905)   He claims to be his cleric and of his see.
It is forbidden by law to judge another's cleric;
for it I could be denounced later.

---

4. See the trial in *El libro de buen amor*, vv. 321-71.

742   But I pronounce this sentence, that he be banished.[5]
(906) If he is found in any part of this see,
       then he is to be strung up, hung from a tree,
       and anyone who pardons him is to be excommunicated."

743   Never again did they see him after they sent him off.
(907) Never did they report him in the entire bishopric.
       They saved the new miracle well,
       and put it in the book with the others.

744   May You, Glorious Mother, always be praised.
(908) You Who know how to give to the evil ones a bad punishment
       and how to honor the good as a judicious person.
       For this you are called Mother, full of grace.

745   You took the evil ones who came to affront your convent
(909) as prisoners inside of your chapel.
       For the good man who wanted to kiss your wimple,
       you duly unfastened it for him, as the document tells.

746   Blessed Lady, Consummate Queen,
(910) crowned by the hand of Christ, Your Son,
       free us from the Devil, from his trap
       that sets an evil ambush for the soul.

747   You guide us Lady, in the lawful life,
(911) you win for us, in the end, a good and perfect destiny.
       Guard us from evil blows and from falling into sin
       so that in the end, our souls may have a good departure.
       (Amen).

---

5. Many scholars, including John E. Keller, read this word as *açotado*, meaning "beaten."

❖ MIRACLE 25 (24)
The Miracle of Theophilus

748   I wish to speak to you about the case of Theophilus,
(703)[1] so beautiful a miracle is not to be forgotten,
       for in it we can understand and believe
       the Glorious One protects those who know how to pray to Her.

749   I would not want, if I could, to prolong the story
(704) for you would be bored and I could err.
       God is customarily pleased with the short prayer,
       may the Creator allow us to make use of it.

750   There was a good man of great wealth
(705) who was called Theophilus as the text says.
       He was a peaceful man; he did not like contention.
       And he knew very well how to control his carnal nature.

751   In the place where he was, he held great authority;
(706) he held the vicarage of his lord the bishop.
       He had superiority over those in the church,
       after the bishop, he was next in command.

752   He was himself a man of good bearing;
(707) he knew how to be at peace and in good agreement with
           everyone.
       He was a temperate man, a man of great knowledge;
       he was very gifted with intelligence and wisdom.

753   He clothed the naked, fed the hungry,
(708) welcomed the pilgrims who came cold;
       he gave good advice to those who erred,
       that they should repent of all their failings.

---

1. The numbering of this miracle tale follows Dutton.

754   The bishop did not have a bother or care,
(709)   except singing his Mass and praying his psalter;
      Theophilus relieved the bishop from all his work,
      to tell of all his goodness would make a long story.

755   The bishop loved him very much,
(710)   for Theophilus freed him from all obligation.
      The towns and people considered him a beacon,
      since he was for everyone the leader and the way.

756   When the time came for him [the bishop] to die,
(711)   the bishop could not live beyond the appointed moment;
      he became ill and died; he went to rejoice with God.
      May God give him Paradise, one should so pray.

757   The people of the land, all the clergy,
(712)   everyone said, "Let Theophilus have the bishopric,
      we understand superiority lies in him.
      It is fitting that he have the command."

758   They sent their letters to the archbishop,
(713)   for God's sake, let him not change his mind from
        Theophilus;
      for they all considered it the soundest advice.
      Anything else would be winter; this would be summer.

759   Those of the archbishopric sent for him.
(714)   They said to him, "Theophilus, take this see,
      since the whole council grants it to you,
      and you are requested by all the communities."

760   Theophilus responded to them with great simplicity:
(715)   "Gentlemen, change your mind for God's sake and for
        charity,
      for I am not so worthy of such an office,
      to make such a choice would be a great blindness."

761   The archbishop said, "I want you to speak,
(716)   I want you to accept this election."
      "Sir," Theophilus said to him, "You will not insist so much
      as to bring me to it willingly."

762   Those of the council, whether it pleased them or not,
(717)   had to make another selection.
      The bishop whom they ordained
      put another vicar in the position.

763 All cases were brought before the new vicar;
(718) the people served Theophilus, but they served him more.
   Theophilus became jealous, the young man worked hard,
   he who was Abel became Cain.

764 In the bishop's house, he was not so favored
(719) as he used to be with the other now passed away.
   He was greatly disturbed in his mind;
   he was beside himself with envy.

765 He considered himself mistreated and ill-fated;
(720) he saw himself disdained by the great and the small.
   He was blinded by indignation and badly disturbed;
   he thought up a wild madness, a truly outrageous error.

766 In that bishopric where Theophilus lived
(721) there was a Jew in that Jewish quarter.
   He knew evil things, every treachery,
   for he had his brotherhood with the Devil.

767 The false trickster was full of evil vices,
(722) he knew enchantments and many machinations.
   The evil one drew circles and did other artifices;
   Beelzebub guided him in all his work.

768 He was very knowledgeable in giving bad advice.
(723) The false traitor carried off many souls;
   as he was the vassal of a very evil lord;
   if ordered to do evil, he did even worse.

769 People thought that he cured by knowledge;
(724) they did not understand that Satan guided it all.
   When by chance he guessed something right,
   the crazy people almost adored him.

770 The Devil had put him in a prominent place;
(725) all came to him asking advice.
   What he said to them, he proved to them.
   He knew how to deceive people in an evil way.

771 All considered him a prophet, young and old,
(726) all ran to him like pigs to acorns.
   Those who were sick, they carried on litters;
   all said, "We will do whatever you command."

772 Wretched Theophilus, forsaken by God,
(727) was conquered by his madness and the promptings of the Devil.

He went to ask advice from the bedeviled trickster:
how he could return to his previous status.

773   The Jew told him, "If you wish to believe me,
(728) you can easily return to what you want.
Have no doubt, if you are steadfast,
all is recovered, if you do not renege."

774   Theophilus answered him like someone drugged,
(729) "For that I came to you, to follow your command."
The Jew told him, "Be assured,
consider that your business is all done.

775   Go enjoy your bed, return to your house,
(730) tomorrow early, while everyone sleeps,
steal away from your men, and from all your household.
Come knock at my door and do nothing else."

776   Theophilus was happy and pleased with this;
(731) he considered his whole business well done.
He returned home greatly deceived;
it would have been better had he stayed there.

777   Then, the next evening, with everyone asleep,
(732) he stole away from his men; he went out of his house.
He went to knock at the door, for he knew the entrance.
The trickster was ready; he opened it without delay.

778   He took him by the hand, in the middle of the night,
(733) and led him out of town to a crossroads.
He told him, "Do not cross yourself or fear anything,
for your whole affair will be improved tomorrow."

779   Soon he saw many great people come
(734) with candelabra and burning candles in hand,
ugly and not shining, with their king in their midst.
Now Sir Theophilus wished he were with his kin!

780   The treacherous trickster took him by the hand;
(735) he brought him to the tent where the master was.
The king received him with sufficient great honor,
as did the princes who were around him.

781   Then the king said to him, "Sir, what do you seek?
(736) I want you to say what brings you here to me
or what man is this that you present to me?
I want to know right away, this you can indeed believe."

782   The Jew said to him, "Lord, crowned king,
(737) this used to be the vicar of the bishopric.
      All loved him very much; he was an honored man.
      Now they have taken it away, whence he is scorned.

783   Therefore he comes to fall at your feet,
(738) so that you may recover for him what he was accustomed
        to have.
      May he do you service with all his might;
      you will have a good vassal in him, in my opinion."

784   The Devil said to him, "It would not be very just
(739) that I seek such profit for another's vassal;
      but let him deny Christ who makes us very hated,
      and I will make his fortune return completely.

785   Let him deny his Christ and Holy Mary,
(740) write me a valid contract to my liking,
      put his seal there at the end,
      and he will return to his rank with great improvement."

786   Theophilus wishing to rise in importance,
(741) had to consent to the pleasure of the Devil.
      He wrote his contract and had it notarized
      with his own seal, which he could not belie.

787   He left him with this and went back to his house,
(742) it was almost cockcrow when he returned.
      No one there was aware of his journey,
      only God from Whom nothing is hidden.

788   But he lost his shadow,[2] he was always without it.
(743) He lost his good color, he remained pale.
      Not due to the power of the Devil but as God willed,
      the unfortunate one returned to his former post.

789   The treacherous one recovered his position;
(744) the bishop knew that he had badly erred.
      He had removed him from the vicarage.
      "Lord," said Theophilus, "may you be pardoned."

790   If before Theophilus had been well liked and loved,

---

2. Dutton (*Obras* 2:234) tells us that according to Menéndez Pidal, it was a general belief that those who had made a pact with the devil lost their shadow. Dutton suggests that *sombra*, or shadow, might also mean peace or well-being.

(745) he was afterwards more served and much more esteemed.
God alone knows, He Who is well informed,
whether it came to him through God or through the Devil.

791 He lived some days in this happy state,
(746) having love and great favor from the bishop,
receiving from people many good gifts,
but in the end Christ wounded him with his lance.

792 This vicar, being in this vicarage,
(747) became very boastful and very daring.
He took to vainglory and great pride;
everyone understood that he was vain.

793 The Lord, Who does not want the death of sinners
(748) but, rather, that souls be saved and errors amended,
made this one sick with mortal pains,
he who was deceived by evil traitors.

794 The good he had done in past times,
(749) the good Lord did not want lost to him.
He resuscitated his mind that lay as dead,
then he opened his eyes, which were asleep.

795 He breathed a little, he regained consciousness,
(750) he considered his case, he saw himself badly manipulated;
he thought deeper about what he had promised.
There Theophilus fell prostrate to the ground.

796 He said to himself, "Wretched, unfortunate one,
(751) from the height where I was, who has knocked me down?
I have lost my soul, scorned my body,
the good that I have lost, I will never see recovered.

797 Wretched sinner, I do not see where to come ashore;
(752) I will not find anyone who wants to pray to God for me.
I will die as one who lies in the middle of the sea
and does not see land to where he can escape.

798 Wretch, poor me, I was born in a bad hour.
(753) I destroyed myself with my own hands, my madness killed
    me.
God had given me a good position,
now I have lost all good fortune.

799 Wretch, although I wish to return to the Glorious One,
(754) Who the scripture says is so merciful,

She will not want to hear me for She is angry with me,
because I denied Her, I did such a disdainful thing.

800 Judas, the traitor, had no greater blame,
(755) he who sold his Lord for a few coins.
I sinned over all others, wretched sinner,
for me there will not be any petitioner.

801 I am lost to God and to Holy Mary,
(756) lost to the saints because of my treachery.
I leveled all the heights where I had a footing;
had I not been born, it would have been much better.

802 On Judgment Day, I, false traitor,
(757) with what face will I come before our Lord?
Everyone will talk about me, wretched sinner.
No one worse than I will come to the assembly.

803 I saw that vicarage at a bad time,
(758) I listened to the Devil, I sought my own dark day.
The trickster, the one of the Jewish quarter, killed me;
he who killed many others with bad advice!

804 I had no needs, nor did I go as a beggar,
(759) everyone did me honor and was pleased with me;
but I went to ask for better than wheat bread.
I looked for my own knife; I was my own enemy.

805 I had something to wear and something to put on my feet.
(760) I had enough for myself; I had enough to give
but, on a dark day, I went to seek an agreement.
I ought to kill myself with my own hands.

806 Indeed I know that I will not be able to end this fever.
(761) There is no doctor or physic who can help me,
save Holy Mary, Star of the Sea,
but who would dare to go to Her begging?

807 I, stinking wretch who smells more than a dog,
(762) a dog that lies rotting, not one that eats bread.
She will not want to hear me, this I know full well,
since I was, against Her, stupid and villainous.

808 Let me appoint the saints as intercessors,
(763) since they are all informed of my bad action.
The martyrs and all the confessors are angry with me,
much more so the apostles, who are even greater.

809 But I do not want to abandon the head for the feet,
(764) I want to approach the Glorious Mother.
I will fall at Her feet, in front of Her altar,
waiting for Her grace, there I want to die.

810 There I will fast, I will do penance,
(765) I will weep, I will say prayers,
I will mortify my flesh, food for worms,
so that She will notice me at some season.

811 Although I denied her like a crazy fool,
(766) I was deceived by a false Jew,
steadfastly I believe, I trust in Her mercy,
from Her was born Christ Who was my Savior.

812 If I go to Her temple tomorrow, very early,
(767) will it happen to me as it happened to the Egyptian,[3]
who suffered great scorn as a bad woman,
until the Glorious One was an intermediary for her.

813 Although God in His mercy may allow me
(768) to go in to see His Majesty,
lightning or fire or some other storm will come
and do harm to many because of my wickedness.

814 Even if God allows me to do all this,
(769) even if he allows me to relate my affliction in peace,
I cannot imagine with what words to begin,
nor do I imagine how I can open my mouth."

815 He abandoned his house and all he had,
(770) he did not tell anyone what he wanted to do.
He went to the church of the place where he lived,
weeping as much as he could.

816 He threw himself at the feet of the Holy Queen,
(771) who is Godmother and Counsel of sinners.
"Lady," he said, "help my wretched soul,
to Your mercy I come seeking medicine.

817 Lady, I am lost and I am abandoned.
(772) I wrote a bad contract and I am badly deceived.

---

3. Santa María Egipciaca (354?-431?), known in English as Saint Mary of Egypt. A penitent harlot who became a saint, she, like Saint Mary Magdalene, is a model of the repentent sinner.

I gave, I know not how, my soul to the Devil;
now I understand that I made a bad bargain.

818   Blessed Lady, Crowned Queen,
(773) Who always prays for wayward people,
       do not make me go rejected from Your house,
       otherwise some will say that You no longer have power.

819   Lady, You Who are the Door of Paradise,
(774) in Whom the King of Glory put so many blessings,
       Lady, turn Your beautiful face to me,
       for I am very repentant of the contract.

820   Turn towards me, Mother, Your beautiful face,
(775) if You are angry with me, You are justified.
       Let not this affair go any further;
       turn to Theophilus, Glorious Queen."

821   Forty days he continued this plea,
(776) he suffered great tribulation day and night.
       Only of this was he mindful, not of any other thing:
       to call on the Glorious One with a true heart.

822   Because Theophilus persisted in his determination,
(777) it pleased the King of Heaven on the fortieth day;
       the Holy Virgin Mary appeared to him at night.
       She said harsh words to him as one who is angry.

823   She said to him, "What are you doing, wretched man?
(778) You are writing on ice, you are pleading in madness.
       I am fed up with your cause, you cause me great bitterness,
       you are very persistent, you anger beyond measure.

824   You make crazy and ineloquent petitions,
(779) you have denied Us, you looked for another Lord.
       Sir, evil renegade, much worse than Judas,
       I do not know who will petition the Creator for you.

825   I would be ashamed to petition my Son;
(780) I would not dare to begin the speech.
       The One Whom you denied and sought to grieve,
       will not want to hear us or pardon you."

826   "Mother," said Theophilus, "for God and charity,
(781) do not look to my merit, look to Your goodness.
       In all that You say, You tell the whole truth,
       for I am dirty and false and full of evil.

827
(782)

I am repentant, Lady, may penitence avail me;
it saves souls, such is our belief.
It saved Peter[4] who did a great sin,
and cleansed Longinus[5] of a very great violence.

828
(783)

Holy Magdalene,[6] sister of Lazarus,
sinner beyond measure since she was a loose woman,
I tell You the same thing about the Egyptian,
She, One who cures all evil, cured them both.

829
(784)

David, with force, committed three mortal sins,[7]
all ugly and dirty and all cardinal.
He made his penitence with heartfelt moans,
the Father of the penitents pardoned him.

830
(785)

The towns of Nineveh[8] that were condemned
did penance crying for their sins.
All their failings were pardoned;
many would have been destroyed who were saved.

831
(786)

This speech, Lady, is Yours to consider,
doing penance thus should help me.
Mother, if You wished and it were Your pleasure,
this judgment ought not perish in me."

832
(787)

He was quiet after all this. Then Holy Mary spoke,
and She said, "Theophilus, you have a very complicated plea.
Indeed, I would pardon easily My dishonor,
but that of My Son, I truly would not dare to.

833
(788)

Although you denied Me and did a vile deed,
I wish to advise you with true counsel.
Turn to My Son because He is angry with you,
since He considers Himself very mistreated by you.

834
(789)

Pray to Him constantly with very great vehemence,
deny the Devil, confirm your belief.

---

4. Reference to the denial of Saint Peter (Matthew 27.67-75).

5. Longinus is traditionally the centurion present at the crucifixion.

6. Saint Mary Magdalene.

7. David's three sins were the killing of Uriah, his adultery with Bathshebah, and his ordering of the census of the Hebrews (2 Samuel 24).

8. See Jonah 3, Matthew 12.41, and Luke 11.32.

He is very merciful and very knowledgeable,
He kills, He gives life for His is such power."

835   "Mother," said Theophilus, "may You always be praised.
(790) It was like Easter, a great day when You were born.
My soul is greatly comforted with this;
Your word brings proven medicine.

836   I would not dare to implore Your Son.
(791) Because of my bad fortune I sought to grieve Him greatly;
but I trust in Him as I should trust,
and I want to demonstrate my belief to You.

837   I believe that there is one God and that He is Trinity,
(792) Trinity in persons, one the Deity;
there is no diversity in the persons,
Father, Son and Spirit, They are truly One.

838   I believe in the incarnation of Jesus Christ,
(793) Who was born of You Mother for our redemption.
He preached the Gospel, then He suffered the passion,
on the third day He was resurrected.

839   I believe completely in His Ascension,
(794) that He sent the grace of consolation.
I believe in the last regeneration,
when good and bad will receive their reward.

840   Mother, I believe it all, I am very certain of it,
(795) of everything Christ orders a Christian to believe;
but I am in great shame, in very great fear,
for I was, my Lady, very villainous to Him.

841   A bad and dirty man, falsely witnessed,
(796) He will not want to hear me because it is not fitting.
Mother, I fear so much that I will be repudiated;
our plea will end up very damaged.

842   If it is to turn out well, or You want to help me,
(797) You must work on this matter, Mother.
Do not order me to search for another intercessor,
since no matter how much I may search, I will not find one.

843   You are helpful in everything, thanks to the Creator!
(798) For beseeching Your Son, Your Father, Your Lord;
whatever You order and like,
He will do it all for You with great love.

844 What You never did for another sinner,
(799) do it not for Theophilus, but for Our Lord.
   Return me to the grace of Your Holy Flower,
   the Flower that You bore without stain or pain.

845 Blessed Lady, Illustrious Queen,
(800) even though it is audacious, I wish to tell You something else:
   if I do not recover the letter I wrote in my wickedness,
   I will not consider myself free from the evil noose."

846 Holy Mary said, "Sir Dirt, Sir Evil,
(801) the letter you wrote with your wicked leader,
   that later you sealed with your own seal,
   lies in a small corner of Hell.

847 My Son will not want, on account of your plight,
(802) to undertake such a pilgrimage, descending to Hell,
   since it is a stinking place, with a foul-smelling gang.
   It would be very daring just to suggest it to Him."

848 "Lady, blessed among all women,
(803) Your Son will want what You want.
   He will give You everything that You request;
   the letter will come to me if You so favor.

849 Wherever the devil has put it,
(804) if He only wishes, then it will be returned.
   Lady, you are the health and life of all,
   I cannot beg You more nor do I know what more to ask of
    You."

850 Holy Mary, Proven Good Comfort, said to him,
(805) "Be in peace, Theophilus. I see you very disconsolate.
   I will go, if I can, to carry out the errand.
   May God order it done quickly!"

851 The Blessed Mother, having given this speech,
(806) took herself away from him and he could not see anything;
   but his will was comforted,
   for Her solace is proven medicine.

852 If Theophilus was very devoted before,
(807) after this he was even more remorseful.
   Three days and three nights he was in prayer;
   he neither ate, nor drank, nor left off reading.

853 His eyes resembled two perennial fountains,

(808)   he hit his head against the hard stones;
        his fists gave his chest great blows.
        He said, "Help me Mother, as You help others!

854   Help me, Holy Mother, hear my cries,
(809)   You Who do such things and others even greater.
        You know my cares, You understand my pain,
        do not forget me, Mother, Solace of Sinners."

855   Theophilus suffered much during this triduum,
(810)   lying on the ground praying every day.
        Never did a Christian suffer more in as many days;
        in the end his suffering was not in vain.

856   The Queen of Glory, Mother, Holy Mary,
(811)   visited him finally on the third day.
        She brought him greetings, joyous news,
        which everyone who lies in sickness wants.

857   "Know, Theophilus," She said, "that your prayers,
(812)   your great moans, your afflictions,
        have been carried to Heaven with great processions.
        The angels carried them singing sweet sounds.

858   My Son is pleased with your efforts,
(813)   the wrong that you did, you have amended well.
        If you persevere as you have begun,
        your case is well placed and very well executed.

859   I spoke about your plight willingly,
(814)   I bent My knees before the Majesty.
        God has pardoned you. A great charity having been done,
        it is fitting that you be firm in your goodness."

860   "Mother of God, Our Lord," said Theophilus,
(815)   "because of You this comes to me and I am well aware of it.
        You freed from condemnation a sinful soul,
        that would lie in Hell with Judas the traitor.

861   But with all this that You have done,
(816)   still I am unsure, still I am unsatisfied,
        because I do not see the letter nor have I recovered the
          text,
        which I wrote when I had denied Your Son.

862   Mother, had I the recovered letter,
(817)   and saw it burned inside a fire,

even were I to die, I would not care,
since my soul is sorely confused.

863 Mother, indeed I know that You are angry about this matter,
(818) but if You fail me, I have nothing.
Lady, You who have begun this chore,
have the letter returned to me and it will indeed be finished."

864 "It will not be for that reason," said the Glorious One,
(819) "let the matter not be damaged for so little."
The beautiful Queen disappeared from him;
She went hurriedly to search for this letter.

865 Theophilus, who was discouraged, took heart
(820) and no wonder since he was so distressed;
he returned to his study as was his custom.
Never was there in this world a more troubled confessor.

866 He returned to his study, to do his penance,
(821) to be very abstinent in eating and drinking,
maintaining all his belief in the Glorious One,
that God through Her would give him His affection.

867 On the third night he lay asleep;
(822) because he suffered great torment, he was scarcely conscious.
The Glorious One came to him with the errand completed,
quiet and without any noise, his letter in hand.

868 The Wife of Christ, Maiden and Mother,
(823) cast it down to him and it struck him.
Sir Theophilus awoke, from death he returned to life,
finding in his lap the cursed letter.

869 With this Theophilus was happy and proud,
(824) he saw the letter returned to his hand.
There he found that he was well cured of the fever.
He held tight to the letter and fulfilled his triduum.

870 Theophilus, the confessor, was very happy
(825) when he held the letter in his power.
He gave thanks to Christ and to Holy Mary,
for She had taken care of his problem.

871 He said, "Good Lady, may You always be praised,
(826) may You always be blessed, always glorified.
To sinners You are well proven,
since never was there born another so sweet or so helpful.

872 May You always be blessed, may Your Fruit be praised.
(827) Holy is Your name, holier is His.
You took me out, Mother, of the bedeviled well,
where always, without end, I would lie drowned.

873 Blessed Lady, Holy Mother Mary,
(828) I cannot tell You how much I thank You.
Mother, give me intelligence, wisdom, and knowledge
with which I may praise You, for I would do so gladly.

874 Powerful Queen of honored deeds,
(829) Who always works to save the wayward,
attain for me pardon from my sins,
so that I may praise Your great good with dignity.

875 Mother of the King of Glory, out of pity,
(830) purify my lips and my will,
so that I may worthily praise Your goodness,
for You have done exceedingly great charity for me."

876 The next day, after this had happened,
(831) when the Glorious Mother had brought the letter,
was Sunday, a wonderful celebration,
when the Christian people all go about joyously.

877 The entire population came to hear Mass,
(832) to take the blessed bread, to receive the holy water.
The bishop of the town wanted to say Mass;
the good man wanted to fulfill his office.

878 Theophilus, the confessor, a penitent Christian,
(833) went to the church with his letter in hand.
He prostrated himself at the feet of the celebrant;
he confessed the whole from beginning to end.

879 He made his confession, pure and true,
(834) how he led his life from an early age,
then how envy, which had taken him from the path,
had blinded him in a strange way.

880 How he went to the Jew, a bad-tempered trickster,
(835) how he had given him dirty and unjust advice,
how he had drawn up a pact with the Devil,
and how the agreement was confirmed by a letter.

881 How through the Glorious One he had recovered that
letter,

(836) the one he had sealed with his seal.
He did not leave out a detail, small or large,
until he had told it all and why it had happened.

882   He showed the letter that he held in his fist,
(837) in which all the force of the bad pact lay.
The bishop who saw this thing crossed himself;
the matter was so enormous that he hardly believed it.

883   *Ite missa est* said, the Mass ended
(838) and everyone was anxious to leave.
The bishop made the sign of the cross with his holy hand,
and all the people remained as they had stood.

884   He said, "Hear, gentlefolk, of a great event:
(839) never in this world will you hear of one so great.
You will see how the Devil uses evil tricks;
he badly deceives those who do not guard themselves from
     him.

885   This our canon and our companion,
(840) moved by his madness and by a false adviser,
went to seek the wise and crafty Devil,
to recover the office he held before.

886   He knew how to deceive, the false traitor;
(841) he told him to deny Christ, his Lord,
and Holy Mary, who was a good Sister,
and then he would return him to all his honor.

887   This wretched sinner agreed to it,
(842) he entered into a pact with him, this was the worst;
he corroborated that work with his own seal.
Lord, Our God, guard us from such a friend.

888   God who always desires the health of sinners,
(843) who suffered great pain to save us,
did not want such works to be fruitful,
for they were plowed by evil farmers.

889   If the Glorious Virgin had not availed him,
(844) the unhappy one would surely have been led astray,
but Her Holy Grace has now helped him.
She has recovered the letter; if not, he would be lost.

890   I hold it in my fist, you can see it,
(845) there is no doubt here; you must believe.

We must then all give thanks to God
and to the Holy Virgin who deigned to help him."

891　All rendered thanks, women and men,
(846)　they proffered many lauds and great processions,
　　　weeping greatly, saying prayers
　　　to the Glorious Mother, good in all seasons.

892　The "Te Deum laudamus" was sung loudly;
(847)　"Tibi laus, tibi gloria" was repeated well.
　　　They said "Salve Regina"; they sang it with gusto
　　　and other songs sweet of sound and word.

893　Then the bishop ordered a great fire built,
(848)　the people seeing it, since it was in the church,
　　　threw that letter into the flames.
　　　It burned; parchment and wax became ash.

894　As soon as the people had made their invocation,
(849)　the letter was burned, thanks to the Creator!
　　　The holy confessor received *Corpus Domini*,
　　　with all the people present seeing it.

895　Immediately afterward, Theophilus, a martyred body,
(850)　received *Corpus Domini* and was fully confessed.
　　　He was surrounded by brightness in sight of the people,
　　　by a splendor so great it could not be imagined.

896　People were certain that he was a holy man,
(851)　and that he, for whom God did so much, was of great merit,
　　　and God covered him with such a beautiful cloak,
　　　from which the Devil took great offense.

897　His face was shining, emitting rays of light,
(852)　like Moses when he carried the Law,
　　　or like Saint Andrew when he was on the cross;
　　　with this the Creator was giving him no small honor.

898　When the town and the people saw this,
(853)　such shining rays issuing from his face,
　　　they sang other lauds and other prayerful songs.
　　　All were ardent in praising the Glorious One.

899　Theophilus so persisted in his contemplation
(854)　that vainglory did not move him, nor did pride take hold.
　　　He returned to the church where he had seen the vision,
　　　never before was he more devout

900
(855)
The good man understood, God made him certain,
that his last day was soon drawing near.
He divided what he had, no money was left,
he gave it all to the poor, he made a good planting.

901
(856)
He asked for pardon from those of the neighborhood;
they all pardoned him willingly.
He kissed the hand of the bishop; he acted correctly;
he died on the third day; God granted him mercy.

902
(857)
He lived only three days after receiving communion,
and since the document had turned to ash.
He died in the church where he had been visited;
in this same place his body was buried.

903
(858)
Thus died Theophilus, the fortunate.
The error he committed, may God be praised,
he completely rectified; he pleased God.
The Glorious One was helping him, may She be much
    thanked.

904
(859)
Gentlefolk, such a miracle as we have heard,
we must never cast into oblivion.
Otherwise, we will all be of bad conscience,
we who have no common sense or perfect wisdom.

905
(860)
So says Saint Paul,[9] the good preacher,
who was a loyal vassal of God, Our Lord,
that all lessons are the Creator's,
all preach the salvation of man the sinner.

906
(861)
From this story we understand and appreciate
how much penitence is worth to the one who knows how
    to use it.
If not for it, you could swear,
Sir Theophilus would have gone to a bad place.

907
(862)
Had the Glorious Mother, Who deigned to help him,
not understood him, She would not have come to see him.
Whoever wishes to listen and to believe me,
let him live in penitence and he may be saved.

908
(863)
Friends, if you wish to save your souls,
if you wish to take my advice,

---

9. See Romans 15.4.

make your confessions, do not delay,
and take penance and think about how to keep it.

909 Jesus Christ wants it, as does the Glorious Virgin,
(864) without Whom no good thing is done,
thus let us endure this sorrowful life,
so that we may gain the lasting and luminous one. (Amen).

910 The Glorious Mother, Queen of Heaven,
(865) Who was for Theophilus such an excellent Godmother,
may She be a help for us in this wretched world
so that we cannot fall into evil ruin. (Amen).

911 Mother, be mindful of Your Gonzalo
(866) who was the versifier of all Your miracles.
Pray for him, Lady, to the Creator,
since Your privilege helps the sinner.
Win for him the grace of God, Our Lord. (Amen).

Selected Bibliography

Editions

Beltrán, Vicente, ed. *Milagros de Nuestra Señora.* 3d ed. Barcelona: Planeta, 1990.

Bolaño e Isla, Amancio, ed. *Milagros de Nuestra Señora. Vida de Santo Domingo de Silos. Vida de San Millán de la Cogolla. Vida de Santa Oria. Martirio de San Lorenzo.* Modern version with prologue. México: Porrúa, 1965.

Devoto, Daniel, ed. *Milagros de Nuestra Señora.* Modern version. Odres Nuevos. Madrid: Castalia, 1969.

Dutton, Brian, ed. *Los Milagros de Nuestra Señora de Gonzalo de Berceo.* 2d ed. Vol. 2 of *Obras completas* of Gonzalo de Berceo. London: Támesis, 1980.

Gerli, Michael, ed. *Milagros de Nuestra Señora.* 4th ed. Madrid: Cátedra, 1989.

Hämel, A., ed. *Milagros de Nuestra Señora.* Halle: Niemeyer, 1926.

Janer, Florencio, ed. *Los Milagros de Nuestra Señora.* In *Biblioteca de Autores Españoles.* Vol. 57. Madrid: Real Academia Española, 1852. 103-31.

Marden, C. Carroll, ed. *Berceo: Veintitrés milagros: Nuevo manuscrito de la Real Academia Española. Revista de Filología Española.* Anejo X. Madrid: Real Academia Española, 1929.

———, ed. *Cuatro poemas de Berceo. Revista de Filología Española.* Anejo IX. Madrid: Real Academia Española, 1928.

———, ed. *Veintitrés milagros: Nuevo manuscrito de la Real Academia Española.* Madrid: Hernando, 1929.

Matus Romo, Eugenio, ed. *Milagros de Nuestra Señora.* Modern version with prologue and notes. Santiago de Chile: Universitaria, 1956.

Montoya Martínez, Jesús, ed. *El libro de los Milagros de Nuestra Señora.* Granada: Universidad de Granada, 1986.

Narbona, A., ed. *Milagros de Nuestra Señora.* Madrid: Alce, 1984.

Sánchez, Tomás Antonio, ed. *Colección de poesías castellanas anteriores al siglo XV*, vol. 2. Madrid: A. de Sancha, 1780.

Solalinde, Antonio [García], ed. *Milagros de Nuestra Señora.* 6th ed. Clásicos Castellanos 44. Madrid: Espasa-Calpe, 1964.

Baro, José. *Glosario completo de los "Milagros de Nuestra Señora" de Gonzalo de Berceo.* Boulder: Society of Spanish and Spanish-American Studies, 1987.

Baldwin, Spurgeon. "Narrative Technique in Gonzalo de Berceo." *Kentucky Romance Quarterly* 23 (1976): 17-28.

Bartha, J.K. "Four Lexical Notes on Berceo's *Milagros de Nuestra Señora.*" *Romance Philology* 37 (1983): 56-62.

———. *Vocabulario de los "Milagros de Nuestra Señora" de Gonzalo de Berceo.* Normal, Ill.: Applied Literature Press, 1980.

Beltrán, Luis. "Between Poetry and the Play: Possible Traces of a Lost Theatre." In *Los hallazgos de la lectura: Estudio dedicado a Miguel Enguídanos*, ed. John Crispin, Enrique Pupo-Walker, and Luis Lorenzo-Rivero. Madrid: Porrúa Turanzas, 1989.

Bermejo-Cabrero, José Luis. "El mundo jurídico en Berceo." *Revista de la Universidad de Madrid*, nos. 70-71 (1969), Homenaje a Menéndez Pidal II, 33-52.

Boreland, Helen. "Typology in Berceo's *Milagros*: The *Judiezno* and the *Abadesa preñada.*" *Bulletin of Hispanic Studies* 60 (1983): 15-29.

Boubée, Joseph. "La poésie mariale. Gonzalo de Berceo (1198?-1260?)." *Etudes des Pères de la Compagnie de Jésus* (Paris) 90 (1904): 512-36.

Buceta, Erasmo. "Un dato para los *Milagros* de Berceo." *Revista de Filología Española* 9 (1922): 400-2.

Burkard, Richard. "Narrative Art and Narrative Inconsistency in Berceo's *Milagro* of the Shipwrecked Pilgrim." *Romanistisches Jahrbuch* 40 (1989): 280-91.

———. "Revenge of a Saint or Revenge of the Deity? Ambiguousness in Five of Berceo's Mary Legends." *Romanistisches Jahrbuch* 37 (1986): 251-63.

———. "Two Types of Salvation in Berceo's *Milagros de Nuestra Señora.*" *Hispanic Journal* 9 (spring 1988): 23-35.

Burke, James F. "The Ideal of Perfection: The Image of the Garden-Monastery in Gonzalo de Berceo's *Milagros de Nuestra Señora.*" In *Medieval, Renaissance and Folklore Studies in Honor of John Esten Keller*, ed. Joseph R. Jones. Newark, Del.: Juan de la Cuesta, 1980. 20-38.

Cabada Gómez, Manuel. "La metafábula." *Senara: Revista de Filoloxia* 1 (1979): 151-70.

Campo, Agustín del. "La técnica alegórica en la introducción de los

Milagros de Nuestra Señora." Revista de Filología Española 28 (1944): 15-57.

Capuano, Thomas. "Agricultural Elements in Berceo's Descriptions of Hayfields." *Hispania* 69.4 (1986): 808-12.

———. "*Semencero* in Berceo's *Milagros.*" *Journal of Hispanic Philology* 8 (1984): 233-38.

Carrizo Rueda, Sofía. "Textos de la clerecía y de la lírica cortesana y la cuestión de 'lo oficial' y 'lo popular.'" *Revista de Dialectología y Tradiciones Populares* 44 (1989): 27-39.

Castro, Américo. "Gonzalo de Berceo." In *La realidad histórica de España.* Mexico: Porrúa, 1954. 341-50.

Cirot, Georges. "L'expression dans Gonzalo de Berceo." *Bulletin Hispanique* 44 (1942): 5-16.

Darbord, Michele. "Los *Milagros de Nuestra Señora* de Berceo: Rhétorique et poésie." *Iberia* 1 (1977): 71-79.

Devoto, Daniel. *Gonzalo de Berceo et la musique. Etudes sur deux mots espagnols anciens.* Paris: La Sorbonne, 1955.

———. "Notas al texto de los *Milagros de Nuestra Señora* de Berceo." *Bulletin Hispanique* 59 (1957): 5-25.

———. "Los ojos de Berceo." *Realidad* (Buenos Aires) 14 (1949): 68-78.

———. "Tres notas sobre Berceo y la historia eclesiástica española." *Bulletin Hispanique* 70 (1968): 261-99.

———. "Tres notas sobre Berceo y la polifonía medieval." *Bulletin Hispanique* 80 (1980): 293-352.

Diz, Marta Ana. "Berceo: La ordalía del niño judío." *Filología* 23.1 (1988): 3-15.

———. *Historias de certidumbre: los "Milagros" de Berceo.* Newark, Del.: Juan de la Cuesta, 1995.

Drayson, Elizabeth. "Some Possible Sources for the Introduction to Berceo's *Milagros de Nuestra Señora.*" *Medium Aevum* 50 (1981): 274-83.

Duarte, Sergio. "Elementos dramáticos en cinco *Milagros de Nuestra Señora* de Berceo." *Duquesne Hispanic Review* 11 (1972): 35-52.

Dutton, Brian. "Berceo's *Milagros de Nuestra Señora* and the Virgin of Yuso." *Bulletin of Hispanic Studies* 44 (1967): 81-87.

———. "The Profession of Gonzalo de Berceo and the Paris Manuscript of the *Libro de Alexandre.*" *Bulletin of Hispanic Studies* 37 (1960): 137-45.

Dyer, Nancy Joe. "A Note on the Use of *verso agudo* in the *Milagros de Nuestra Señora.*" *Romance Notes* 18 (1977): 252-55.

Fernández y González, Francisco. "Berceo, o el poeta sagrado de la España cristiana del siglo XIII." *La Razón* 1 (1860): 222-35, 300-22, 393-402.

Ferrer, José. "Berceo: *Milagros de Nuestra Señora.* Aspectos de su estilo." *Hispania* 33 (1950): 46-50.

Finke, Wayne H. "La imagen de la mujer en *Los Milagros* de Berceo." In *Festschrift for José Cid Pérez*, ed. Alberto Gutiérrez de la Solana and Elio Alba-Buffill. New York: Senda Nueva de Ediciones, 1981. 211-15.

Foresti Serrano, Carlos. "Sobre la Introducción de los *Milagros de Nuestra Señora.*" *Anales de la Universidad de Chile* 107 (1957): 361-67.

García de la Fuente, Olegario. "Sobre el léxico bíblico de Berceo." ed. Claudio Garcia Turza. In *Actas de las III Jornadas de Estudios Berceanos*, Logroño: Instituto de Estudios Riojanos, 1981. 73-89.

Garci-Gómez, Miguel. "La abadesa embargada por el pie." *Revista de Dialectología y Tradiciones Populares* 44 (1989): 7-26.

Gariano, Carmelo. *Análisis estilístico de los "Milagros de Nuestra Señora" de Berceo*, 2d ed. Madrid: Gredos, 1971.

———. "El género literario en los *Milagros* de Berceo." *Hispania* 49 (1966): 740-47.

Garofoli, Bruna. "L'aggettivazione nei *Milagros de Berceo*: L'uomo." In *Actas del Congreso Internacional sobre la lengua y la literatura en tiempos de Alfonso X*, ed. Fernando Carmona and Francisco J. Flores. Murcia: Facultad de Letras, Universidad de Murcia, 1985. 239-56.

Garrido Gallardo, M.A. "Una clave interpretativa para tres *recursos literarios* fundamentales en los *Milagros de Nuestra Señora.*" *Revista de Filología Española* 59 (1977): 279-84.

Gerli, E. Michael. "La tipología bíblica y la introducción de los *Milagros de Nuestra Señora.*" *Bulletin of Hispanic Studies* 62 (1985): 7-14.

———. "Poet and Pilgrim: Discourse, Language, Imagery, and Audience in Berceo's *Milagros de Nuestra Señora.*" In *Hispanic Medieval Studies in Honor of Samuel G. Armistead*, ed. E. Michael Gerli and Harvey L. Sharrer. Madison: Hispanic Seminary of Medieval Studies, 1992. 140-51.

Gicovate, Bernard. "Notas sobre el estilo y la originalidad de Gonzalo de Berceo." *Bulletin Hispanique* 62 (1960): 5-15.

Giménez Resano, Gaudioso. "Cómo vulgariza Berceo sus fuentes latinas." *Berceo* 94-95 (1978): 17-29.

———. *El mester poético de Gonzalo de Berceo*. Logroño: Instituto de Estudios Riojanos, 1976.

Gimeno Casalduero, Joaquín. "Elementos románicos y su función en el milagro XIV de Berceo: 'La imagen respetada'." In *Estudios en homenaje a Enrique Ruiz-Fornells*, ed. Juan Fernández Jiménez, José Labrador Herraiz, L. Teresa Valdivieso. Erie, PA: Asociación de Licenciados y Doctores Españoles en Estados Unidos, 1990. 259-66

Girón Alconchel, José Luis. "Sobre la lengua poética de Berceo (y

II): El estilo indirecto libre en los *Milagros* y sus fuentes latinas."
Revista de Filología 4 (1988): 145-62.

Goldberg, Harriet. "The Voice of the Author in the Works of Gonzalo de Berceo and in the *Libro de Alexandre* and the *Poema de Fernán González.*" *La Corónica* 8 (1980): 100-12.

González-Casanovas, R.J. "Marian Devotion as Gendered Discourse in Berceo and Alfonso X: Popular Reception of the *Milagros* and *Cantigas.*" *Bulletin of the Cantigueiros de Santa María* 4 (spring 1992): 17-31.

Guillén, Jorge. *Language and Poetry.* Clinton, MA: Colonial Press, 1961.

Gutiérrez-Lasanta, F. "Gonzalo de Berceo, cantor de la Gloriosa." *Berceo* 5 (1950): 733-47.

Kantor, Sofía. "Un Récit a dominante modale-Illocutoire: 'El clérigo simple' de Gonzalo de Berceo." *Strumenti Critici* 41 (1980): 60-91.

Keller, John E. "The Enigma of Berceo's *Milagro XXV.*" *Symposium* 29 (1975): 361-70.

———. *Gonzalo de Berceo.* Twayne World Authors Series 187. New York: Twayne, 1972.

———"A Medieval Folklorist." *Folklore Studies in Honor of Arthur Palmer Hudson,* Special issue of *North Carolina Folklore* 13.1-2 (1965): 19-24.

———. "On the Morality of Berceo, Alfonso X, Don Juan Manuel and Juan Ruiz." In *Homenaje a don Agapito Rey,* ed. Josep Roca Pons. Bloomington: Dept. of Spanish and Portuguese, Indiana University, 1980. 117-30.

———. *Pious Brief Narrative in Medieval Castilian and Galician Verse: From Berceo to Alfonso X.* Lexington: University Press of Kentucky, 1978.

Kelley, Mary Jane. "Spinning Virgin Yarns: Narrative, Miracles and Salvation in Gonzalo de Berceo's *Milagros de Nuestra Señora.*" *Hispania* 74.4 (1991): 814-23.

Kelly, Edith L. "'Fer', 'far', 'facer', 'fazer', in Three Works of Berceo." *Hispanic Review* 3 (1935): 127-37.

Kinkade, Richard. "Sermon in the Round: The *Mester de Clercía* as Dramatic Art." In *Studies in Honor of Gustavo Correa.* Potomac, Md.: Scripta Humanistica, 1986. 127-36.

Kirby, Steven D. "Berceo's *descanto.*" *Hispanic Review* 43 (1975): 181-90.

Lanchetas, Rufino. *Gramática y vocabulario de las obras de Berceo.* Madrid: Rivadeneyra, 1900.

Landa, Luis. "'La deuda pagada' de Rasi a Gonzalo de Berceo." *Sefarad: Revista de Estudios Hebraicos, Sefardíes y de Oriente Próximo* 47 (1987): 81-86.

Lewis, Julie. "La estrella, la sombra y el centro en los *Milagros* de Berceo." *Abside* 37 (1973): 110-19.

Lida, María Rosa. "Estar en (un) baño, estar en un lecho de rosas." *Revista de Filología Española* 3 (1941): 263-70.

Lope Blanch, Juan M. "La expresión temporal en Berceo." *Nueva Revista de Filología Hispánica* 10 (1956): 36-41.

López García, A. "Los códigos sintagmáticos de la narración (a próposito de la originalidad del Teófilo de Berceo)." *Berceo* 91 (1976): 147-66.

López Morales, H. "Los narradores de los *Milagros de Nuestra Señora*." In *Actas de las III Jornadas de Estudios Berceanos*, ed. Claudio García Turza. Logroño: Instituto de Estudios Riojanos, 1981. 101-11.

Loveluck, Juan. "En torno a los *Milagros* de Gonzalo de Berceo." *Atenea* 108 (1951): 669-84.

Lugones, N.A. "A los bonos da trigo, a los malos avena." *Berceo* 93 (1977): 171-79.

Marechal, Leopoldo. "El epíteto peyorativo en Berceo." *Kentucky Romance Quarterly* 21 (1974): 309-16.

Menéndez Peláez, J. "La tradición mariológica en Berceo." In *Actas de las III Jornadas de Estudias Berceanos*, ed. Claudio García Turza. Logroño: Instituto de Estudios Riojanos, 1981. 113-27.

Molina, R.A. "Gonzalo de Berceo y el lenguaje oral." Quaderni Ibero Americani 37 (1969): 8-12.

Montoya Martínez, Jesús. "El alegorismo, premisa necesaria al vocabulario de los *Milagros de Nuestra Señora*." *Studi Mediolatini e Volgari* 30 (1984): 167-90.

———. "El milagro literario hispánico." In *Proceedings of the 10th Louisiana Conference on Hispanic Languages and Literatures*, ed. Gilbert Paolini. New Orleans: Tulane University, 1989. 211-20.

———. "El prólogo de Gonzalo de Berceo al libro de los *Milagros de Nuestra Señora*." *La Corónica* 13.2 (1985): 175-89.

Mount, Richard Terry. "Levels of Meaning: Grains, Bread, and Bread Making as Informative Images in Berceo." *Hispania* 76.1 (1993): 49-54.

———. "Light Imagery in the Works of Gonzalo de Berceo." In *Studies in Language and Literature, Proceedings of the 23rd Mountain Interstate Foreign Language Conference*, ed. Charles Nelson. Richmond: Dept. of Foreign Languages, Eastern Kentucky University, 1976. 425-30.

Nelson, Dana. "Generic vs. Individual Style: The Presence of Berceo in the *Alexandre*." *Revue de Philologie* 29 (1975): 143-84.

Nykl, Alois R. "Old Spanish Terms of Small Value." *Modern Language Notes* 42 (1927): 311-13 and 46 (1931): 166-70.

Perry, T. Anthony. *Art and Meaning in Berceo's "Vida de Santa Oria."* New Haven, Conn.: Yale University Press, 1968.

Prat-Ferrer, Juan José. "Estructura y función de los *Milagros de*

Nuestra Señora de Gonzalo de Berceo." *Dissertation Abstracts* 50. 9 (1990): 2891a-2892a.

Resnick, Seymour. "The Jew as Portrayed in Early Spanish Literature." *Hispania* 34 (1951): 54-58.

Rey, Agapito. "Correspondence of the Spanish Miracles of the Virgin." *Romanic Review* 19 (1928): 151-53.

Rozas, Juan Manuel. "Composición literaria y visión del mundo: *El clérigo ignorante* de Berceo." *Studia Hispanica in honorem Rafael Lapesa*, 3 vols. Madrid: Gredos, 1975. 3:431-52.

Ruiz y Ruiz, Lina A. "Gonzalo de Berceo y Alfonso El Sabio: *Los Milagros de Nuestra Señora* y *Las Cantigas*." *Universidad de San Carlos* (Guatemala) 24 (1951): 22-90.

Salmón, Josefa. "El paisaje en Berceo, Garcilaso y Balbuena: Tres concepciones del universo." *Prismal/Cabral* 7-8 (1982): 57-73.

Saugnieux, Joël. *Berceo y las culturas del siglo XIII.* Logroño: Instituto de Estudios Riojanos, 1982.

Scholberg, Kenneth R. "Minorities in Medieval Castilian Literature." *Hispania* 37 (1954): 203-08.

Snow, Joseph T. "Gonzalo de Berceo and the Miracle of Saint Ildefonso: Portrait of the Medieval Artist at Work." *Hispania* 65 (1982): 1-11.

Sobejano, Gonzalo. "El epíteto en Gonzalo de Berceo." *El epíteto en la lírica española.* Madrid: Gredos, 1956. 185-91.

Solalinde, Antonio García. "Gonzalo de Berceo y el obispo don Tello." *Revista de Filología Española* 9 (1922): 398-400.

Suárez Pallasa, Aquilino. "El templo de la 'Introducción' de los *Milagros de Nuestra Señora* de Gonzalo de Berceo." *Letras* (Organo de la Facultad de Letras y Ciencias Humanas de la Universidad Nacional Mayor de San Marcos) 21-22 (Sept. 1989-Aug. 1990): 65-74.

Vicente García, Luis Miguel. "El milagro XVI de los *Milagros de Nuestra Señora* y la versión latina: Transformación de algunos temas." *Mester* 17 (fall 1988): 21-27.

Vila, Claudio. "Estudio mariológico de los *Milagros de Nuestra Señora* de Berceo." *Berceo* 8 (1953): 343-60.

Wilkins, Heanon. "Dramatic Design in Berceo's *Milagros de Nuestra Señora*." In *Hispanic Studies in Honor of Alan D. Deyermond: A North American Tribute*, ed. John S. Miletich. Madison, Wis.: Hispanic Seminary of Medieval Studies, 1986. 309-24.

———. "La función de los diálogos en los *Milagros* de Berceo." In *Actas del Sexto Congreso Internacional de Hispanistas*, ed. Alan M. Gordon and Evelyn Rugg. Toronto: University of Toronto, 1980. 798-801.

———. "Los romeros y las romerías en *Milagros de Nuestra Señora*." In *Studia Hispanica Medievalia: II Jornadas de Literatura*

Española Medieval, ed. Teresa L. Valdivieso and Jorge H. Valdivieso. Buenos Aires: Universidad Católica de Argentina, 1988. 139-51.

Zamora, Silvia Rosa. "La estructura bipolar y tripartita del milagro XXV de Berceo." *Mester* 17 (fall 1988): 29-37.

Index